Anke Redhead

The Art of Creating with Papier-Mâché

A Workshop for Beginners and Advanced Artists

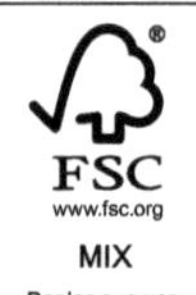

Anke Redhead

The Art of Creating with Papier-Mâché

A Workshop for Beginners

and Advanced Artists

The „Deutsche Nationalbibliothek" registered this publication
in her national bibliography; details are available via internet on
http://dnb.de.

For questions and suggestions please refer to info@papiermache-kunst.de

Published by „Books on Demand, Norderstedt

Publisher: BoD · Books on Demand GmbH, In de Tarpen 42,
22848 Norderstedt, bod@bod.de
Print: Libri Plureos GmbH, Friedensallee 273, 22763 Hamburg

ISBN: 978-3-7693-1997-2

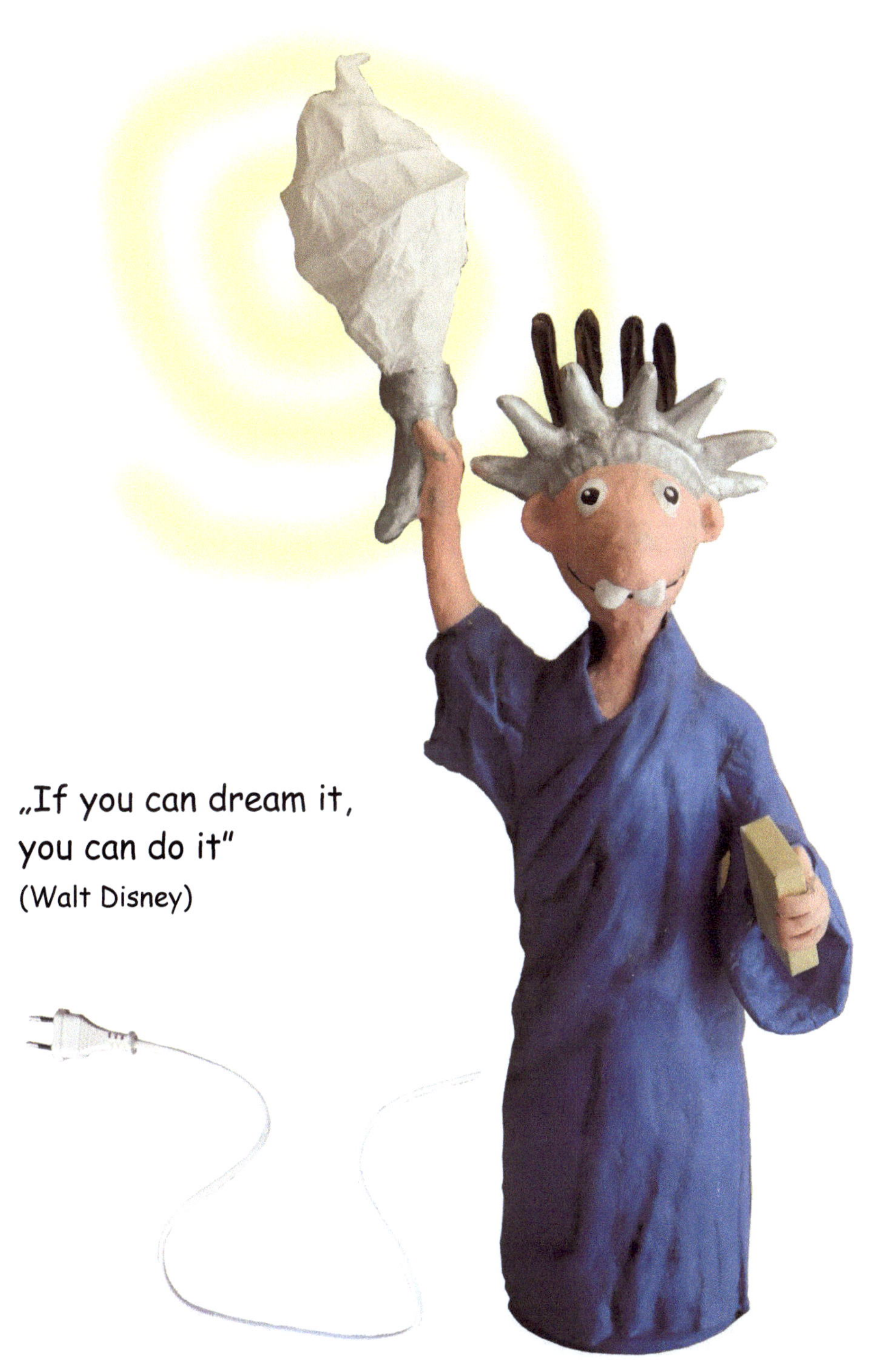

„If you can dream it,
you can do it"
(Walt Disney)

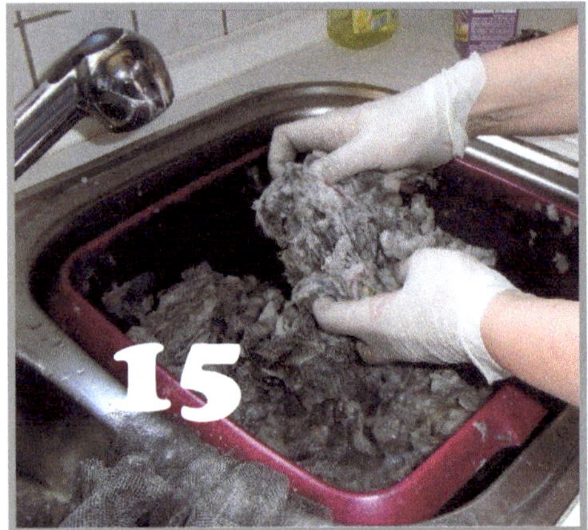

Easily done:

Papier-mâché - quickly crafted using newspaper and glue

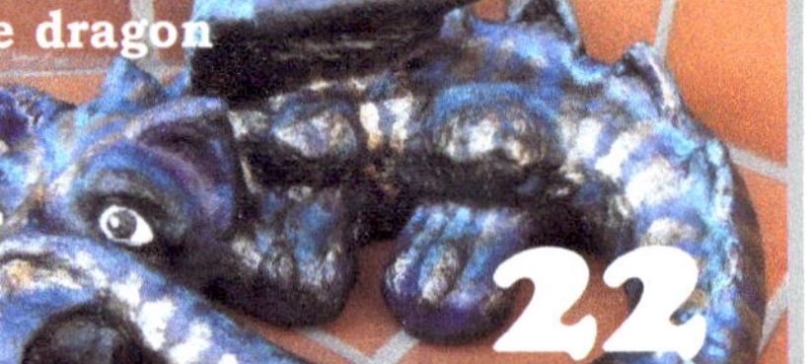

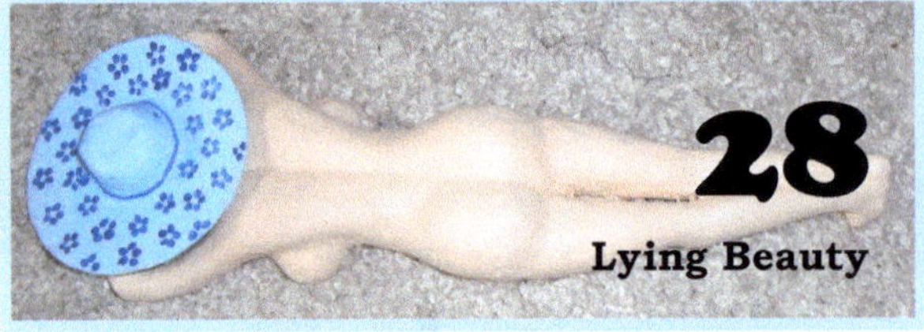

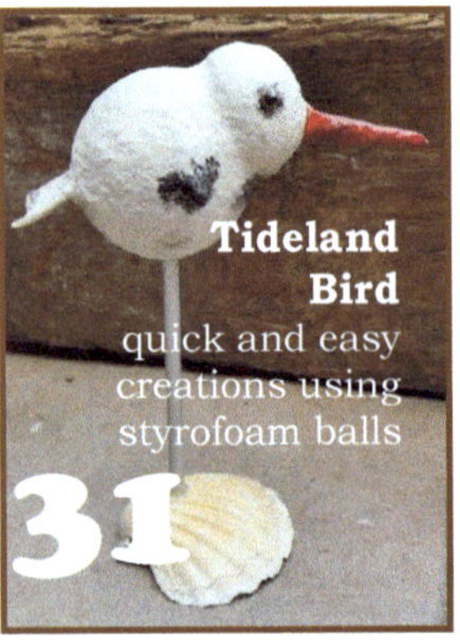

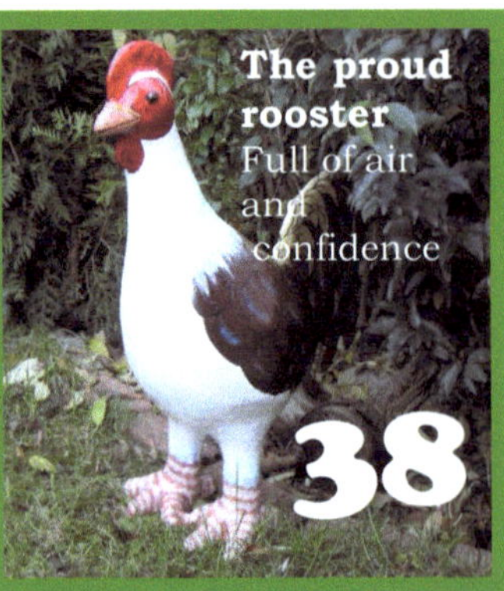

Content

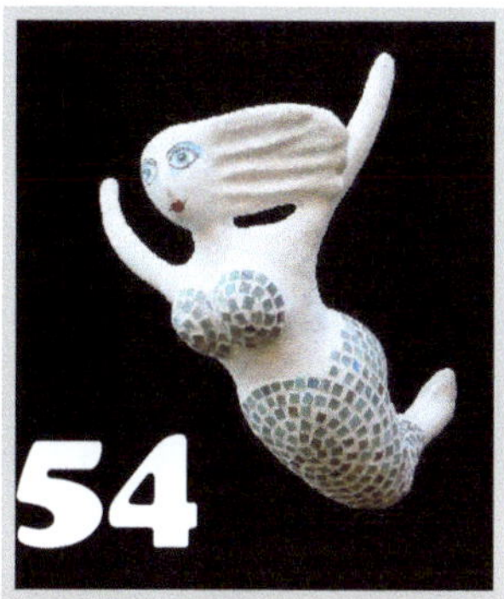

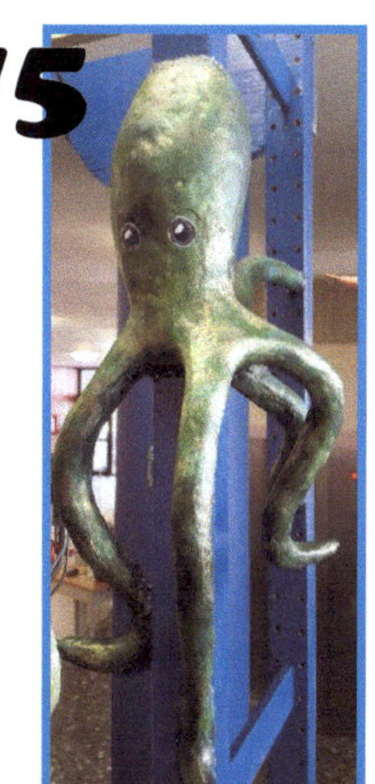

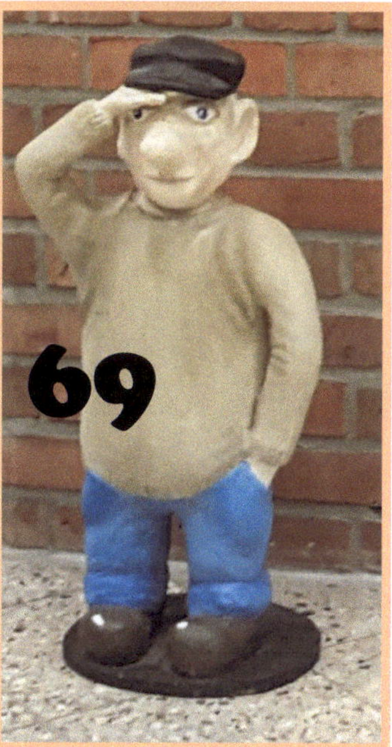

44

The Teacup-table

A very special piece of furniture

Mermaid
Wire construction with papier-mâché and mosaic

54

„Jack", the Sailor

You can do this now:
A sturdy wooden structure supports this brave sailorman

69

75

No limits to your fantasy:

Papier-mâché may easily be applied to a variety of materials, including wood, steel, stone

Be inspired!

Papier-mâché is a very fascinating medium, that can be easily produced and is quite inexpensive and easy to handle. Most of the equipment needed for papier-mâché production can probably be found around your home, with the rest available at a hardware store or craft shop.

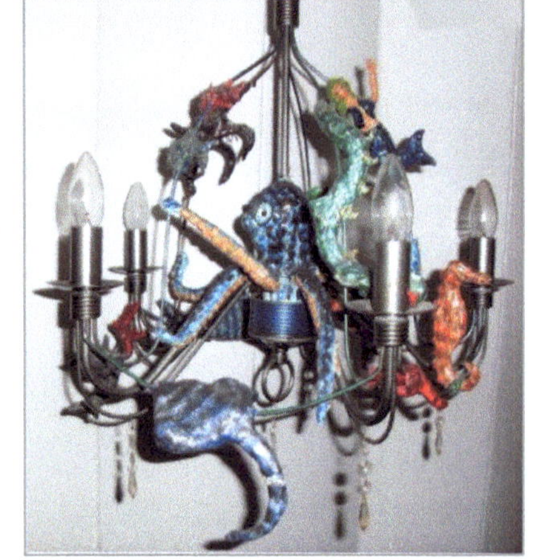

I have been working with papier-mâché for a long time and I am always amazed by the numerous options it offers. Papier-mâché has become increasingly popular in the last few years, partially due to the idea of combining waste recycling with the ability to express your own ideas.

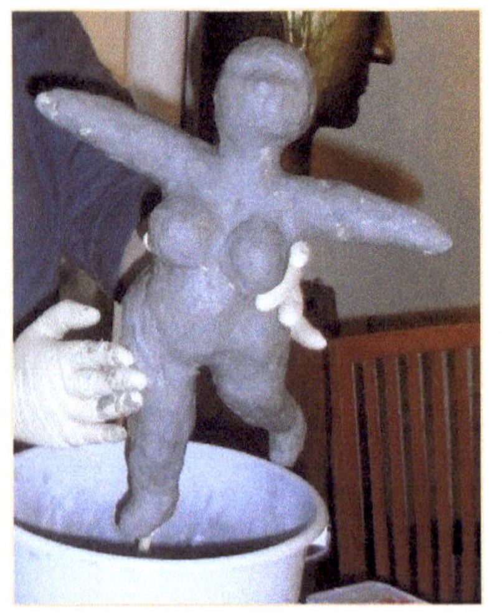

The participants in my papier-mâché workshops are enthusiastic about the fantastic results they can achieve with papier-mâché in an easy and playful way – without any previous knowledge in the field of sculpture. Most of all it is fun and this enthusiasm shows in the completed artwork. Papier-mâché is a perfect material for beginners, advanced learners and artists, alike. During my exhibitions people often ask me how I made my sculptures. They never believe that my material is papier-mâché, as the figures look very solid and of high quality. Questions that are often asked include: "How can I produce such smooth surfaces with papier-mâché?", and "How do I get such great details and textures?", "How do I prepare a solid framework", "How do I create a smooth surface on my sculpture" or "How can I make my figure weather-proof?" These are all achievable through simple techniques and tricks that can be easily learned.

So I decided to share my knowledge and experience, and answer those questions with the help of this book. In my workshops and while creating my own figures, I have collected various ideas, tips and tricks, that I am happy to share. Each project showcases detailed step-by-step instructions, colourful photographs and artworks to inspire your own work!

Instead of being a book full of projects to copy, this book aims to inspire you and provide you with the tools and guidance for your own ideas and projects. All sculptures and objects, which I introduce in this book, serve only as suggestions for developing your own ideas. With this book I invite you to become familiar with the colourful and crazy world of papier-mâché. It is my hope that this book will inspire and guide you to create your own unique pieces and to have fun while doing so.

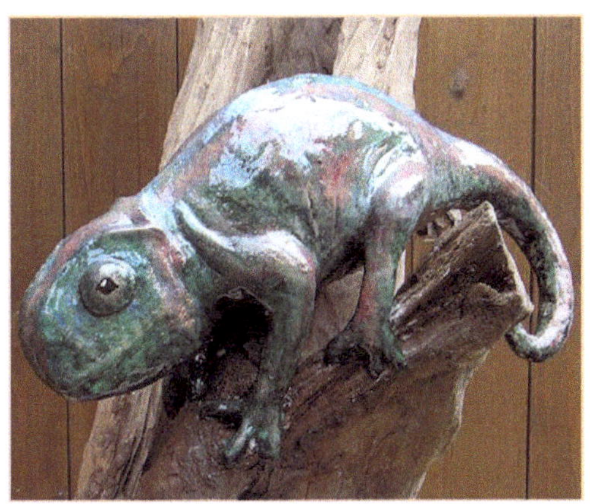

Papier-mâché can easily be made to look like wood, pottery, marble, metal or just like papier-mâché. With the help of different varnishes and paints you can achieve various effects and with the right varnish you can produce a rather waterproof (at least for some years) sculpture.

With papier-mâché you can let your imagination run wild. This is the main message of this book. Don't be too strict or too fussy while creating your papier-mâché figurine. Instead enjoy the creative process and the liveliness of the material.

On the other hand creating with papier-mâché requires a good amount of real handicraft. It involves combining imagination and craftsmanship to produce a unique and personal piece of art. Handicraft is crucial in this process. What good is a beautiful papier-mâché sculpture if it doesn't survive the drying process or ends up with sloping extremities or a dropping head? Therefore, it is essential for me to show you how to create a stable armature with either paper, chicken wire or wood depending on the size of the sculpture. Additionally, I discuss the various possibilities of dealing with the surface of your figure and demonstrate various ways of coating and colouring.

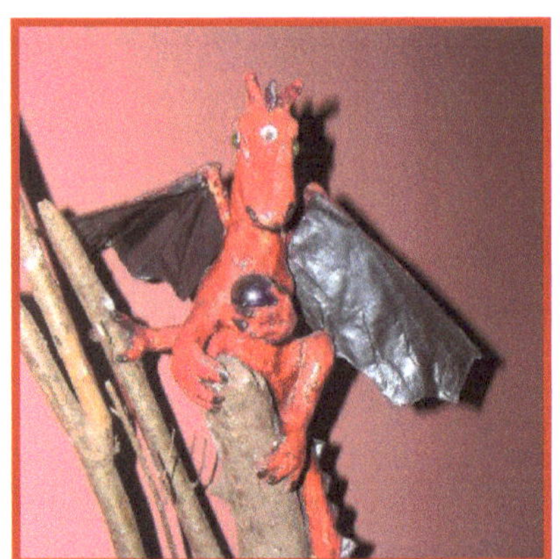

I will guide you to create your individual papier-mâché piece of art, whether it's a slender mermaid, a magnificent dragon or any other unique sculpture you desire. By the end of this book you will not only be able to replicate the presented objects but also adapt the principle of a sturdy base to your own ideas, opening the gateway to a whole world of papier-mâché sculpture-making. Create your figures with freedom and confidence, letting your imagination take the lead. Experiment with new shapes, textures, and techniques, allowing each project to reflect your individuality. This book will inspire you to transform your own ideas into reality, giving life to creations that are uniquely yours.

We will progress from relatively simple figures that require minimal support to chicken-wire-supported objects and, finally, to constructing complex sculptures on wooden substructures. Papier-mâché is an incredibly versatile medium. Whether your creation is small or large, simple or intricate, realistic or fantastical, practical or abstract, the final paint finish is often what defines the expression of the figure. My figures frequently carry a touch of humor, a quality enhanced by papier-mâché's lightness, which makes it, in my view, the perfect medium for creating whimsical, humoristic art. Papier-mâché also has a quirky, unpredictable nature. This ensures that every object you create will be a true original. Even if you attempt to replicate a figure, it will never be identical; it will always bear the unmistakable imprint of your unique style.

I hope this book brings you joy and sparks your creativity, making your papier-mâché journey both fulfilling and delightful.
Have fun and enjoy!

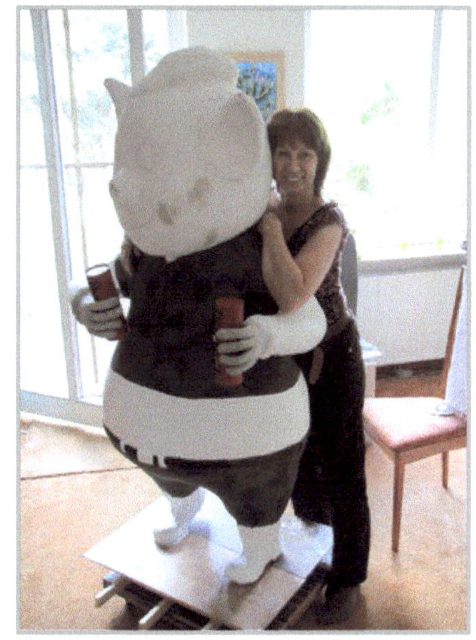

Best regards
Anke Redhead

P.S. This translation was primarily created by a native English-speaking friend from the UK, with certain sections adapted from the German original using AI assistance.

The nature of papier-mâché

Papier-mâché dries easily without an oven

One notable advantage of working with papier-mâché is its ability to dry effortlessly without requiring an oven. Unlike clay or other modelling materials, there's no need for an additional drying process or special equipment. Simply shape your sculpture and allow it to dry naturally in sunlight or at room temperature. Attempting to dry papier-mâché in an oven would only lead to a heap of ashes! All you need is air, which means the size of your creations is not limited by the dimensions of an oven. Fancy building a 1.8-metre-high figure? No problem! With a sturdy substructure and a few buckets of pulp, it's entirely achievable. Accomplishing this with clay, on the other hand, isn't nearly as straightforward, often leading to unpleasant surprises like poor glazing or broken pieces after firing.

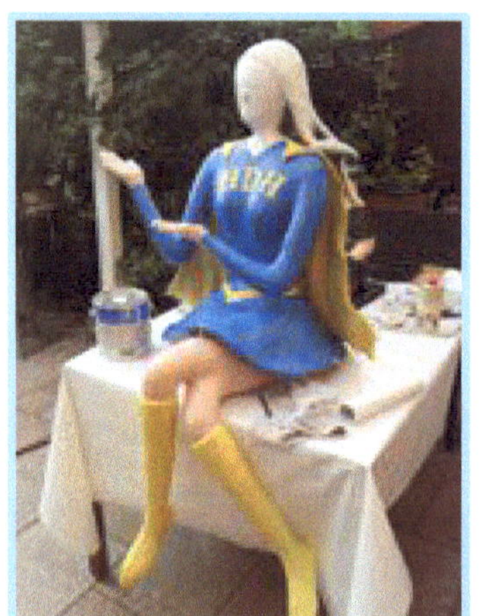

Papier-mâché – a „patient" material

As papier-mâché needs a long time to dry there is no stress, when you are forming your object. This is a great advantage! Even the next day you can still shape the pulp. And even when the figure is completely dry mistakes can still be corrected. When papier-mâché has dried and hardened it has the same properties as wood, so that you can drill a hole, use sandpaper or a saw or attach something with a screw. If you don't like the arm of your figure, just cut it off, attach a new ledger with a screw and make a new arm.

Papier-mâché is friendly towards other materials

It is easy to combine papier-mâché with other materials. You will see later in this book how I form papier-mâché around lamp stands. Roots or furniture can be decorated in the same way. I enjoy strolling around flea markets looking for suitable objects, like rusty weights, old lamp posts or window frames, which I can upgrade with papier-mâché to objects of art. In this way I create amusing lamps, table legs with feet, or combine natural materials like roots with fantasy figures made out of papier-mâché.

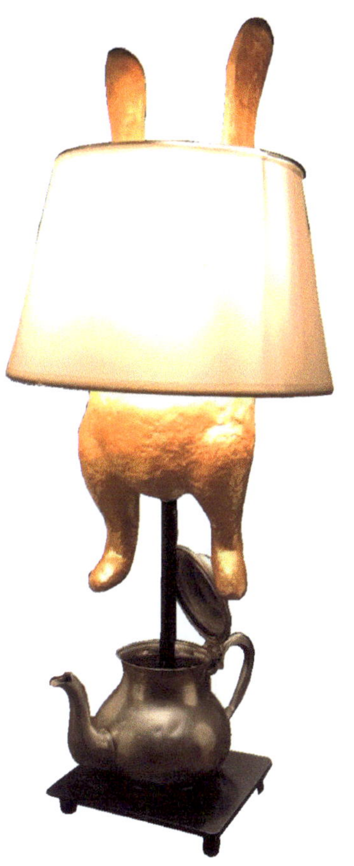

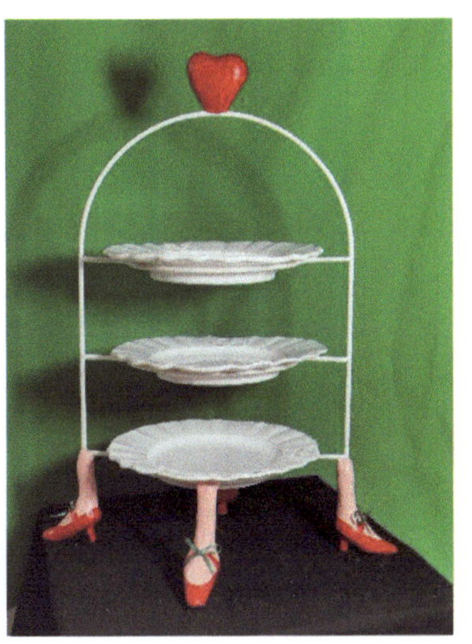

Once you have started down this path you will discover endless possibilities for papier-mâché art by repurposing household objects you no longer need. Have a teapot without a lid? No problem. Fill it up with concrete, insert a pole, and you have a fantastic base for a future figure. This opens up a never-ending range of ideas for our creativity.

Papier-mâché – a low-cost material

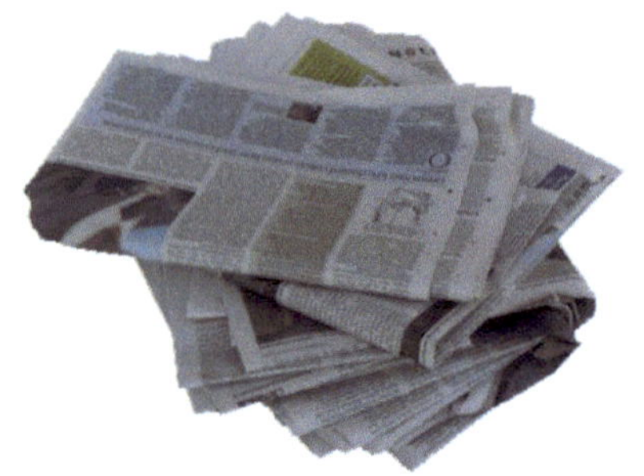

My recipe for creating high-quality papier-mâché starts with using 100% recycled paper. Materials like old newspapers, egg cartons, or even shredded office paper work perfectly. Not only does this approach make your art eco-friendly, but it also adds texture and character to your creations. Let your neighbors and friends know you need such materials for your projects—you'll soon find yourself with an abundance of supplies, perhaps even more than you can use! However, when it comes to glue, don't skimp on quality. Choose a strong adhesive that offers excellent sticking power and a smooth consistency, free of any lumps.

Papier-mâché – a lightweight material

Another advantage of papier-mâché is that once the figures are fully dried, they become remarkably lightweight. I have crafted many large figures, including some that were commissioned and needed to be sent by post. Once the water had evaporated during the drying process, I could easily handle even the larger pieces on my own – something that would have been impossible with concrete. That said, it's worth noting that before drying, papier-mâché figures can be quite heavy due to the high water content in the pulp.

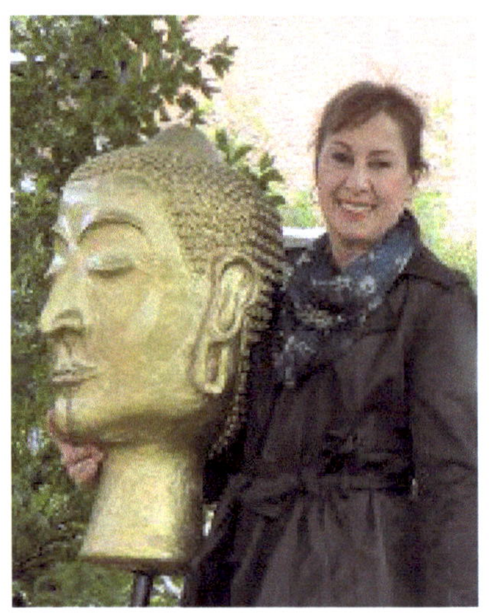

What is special about papier-mâché pulp?

Pulp is produced by shreddering newspaper and mixing it with wallpaper paste and wood glue. All sculptures in this book are made of pulp since it is very productive, inexpensive and robust. And to be honest: I love the kneading part and the feeling of this soft and slushy material.

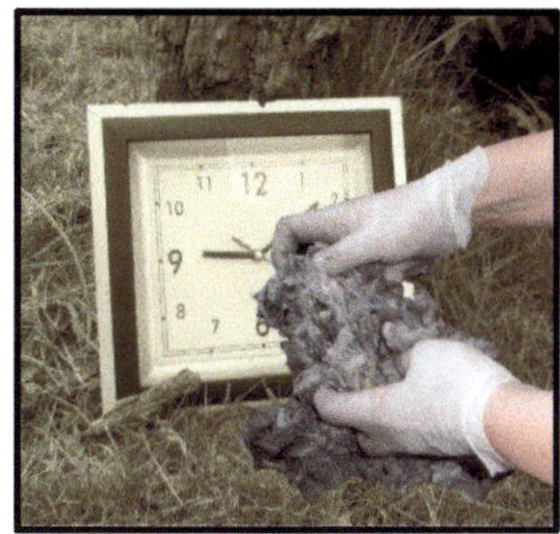

When I was a child I was told to produce papier-mâché in the following way: I tore millions of little strips of newspaper, put them in a pot and mixed it with glue until I had a pulp which was ready to use. It took me about three hours until I had a lump which was the size of a fist. Let us stop with this time consuming method! On page 15 I introduce you to my favorite formula for papier-mâché.

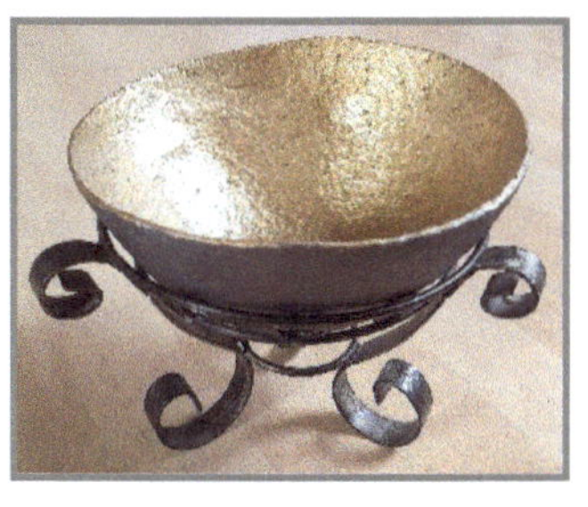

Before I delve into the various types of substructures, here's a quick and simple way to mould objects like plates, bowls or cups using papier-mâché. To create these, I use a household plate or dish, covering it with cling film or coating it lightly with soft soap or Vaseline. Next, I take a tablespoon, apply pulp to its back, and spread it evenly over the chosen surface. It's important to work on the inside of the mould, as drying on the outside may cause cracks to form on the surface of the pulp. The only exception to this rule is when using a balloon, as its softness prevents cracking during the drying process.

Even if cracks occur in your work, they won't ruin it. After the form dries, you can repair the damage by applying fresh papier-mâché and plastering over the cracks. The fresh material will conjoin with the dry material.

Substructure

I need several work processes until my figures are finished. The first step is creating a structure made of wire or wood. For smaller figures, you only need a structure made of firmly scrunched and shaped paper, which is then wrapped with tape to hold it in place. This creates a solid base that is easy to work with. The next step involves applying a layer of pulp across this structure, which serves as the foundational surface. After that, you'll apply a second layer of pulp, focusing carefully on shaping the details. You can mold it with your fingers to refine the figure, but always remember: an internal structure is essential to stabilize the form and maintain its integrity.The first layer will shrink quite substantially as it dries, forming the characteristic bumpy surface of papier-mâché. This happens because the pulp - a mixture of water, newspaper, and glue - loses water during the drying process, causing the compressed newspaper bits to create an uneven texture.

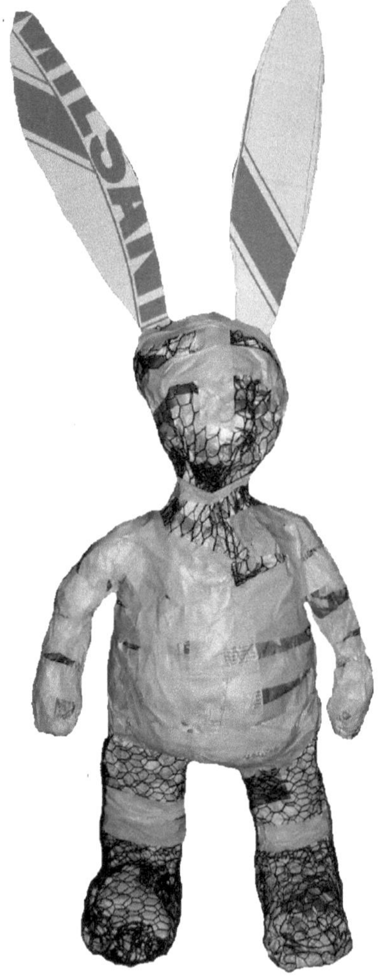

The second layer, applied more thinly, will dry with a much smoother surface, allowing for finer detailing and a polished finish.

How does papier-mâché dry best?

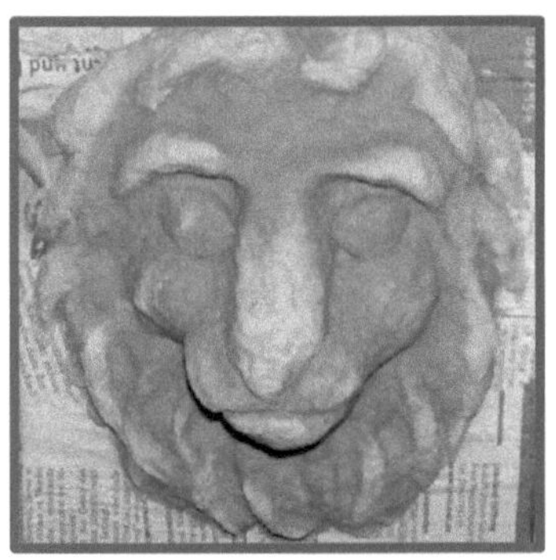

Papier-mâché requires a considerable amount of time to dry, and the drying time is influenced by the temperature in the room and the thickness of the pulp layer. During my early days of working with papier-mâché, I often ruined projects because I applied thick layers of pulp and was misled by the surface appearing to be dry. It may seem dry, but it's not. To avoid this, prepare the inner structure in a way that allows you to apply a pulp layer no thicker than an inch during your first working process. Then, wait until the papier-mâché has thoroughly dried, which may take between one week and ten days.

I know how it feels when a half done figure stares at you and wants to be completed. I also know how your fingers start itching and how you want to varnish and paint the dry figure. Don't do it! Do meditate, eat a yoghurt or have a run, but leave your figure alone until it is completely dry. An early sealing of the surface with varnish or paint interferes with the drying process and in the worst case your figure rots from within.

After your object is thoroughly dry outside, make sure it is turned on its side so that the resting surface (which so far could not dry) will be able to lose its moisture as well. Once the papier-mâché is completely dry it may be primed and painted with almost any paint.

Drying can take a long time. To speed up the drying process you can place your object in front of an electric fan or a sunny window. Recently I tested whether you can dry small papier-mâché objects in the microwave. I have to advise strongly against this, as I nearly burnt down my kitchen. First I set up the microwave at 3 minutes and was happy that the object was quite dry. But when I added another 5 minutes the moisture evaporated very quickly and the object and the whole microwave caught fire.

Storage and durability

Once papier-mâché pulp has been prepared, it's important to use it promptly. When exposed to air, the pulp hardens quickly, rendering it unusable after about a week. To extend its lifespan, store it in an airtight container; this way, it can last for several weeks. Beyond this point, the pulp will begin to emit an unpleasant odor, and the wallpaper paste within it will lose its adhesive properties. For optimal storage, consider using a bucket lined with a sturdy plastic bag. Pour the pulp into the bag, then securely seal it whenever it's not in use to limit air exposure. Storing the pulp in the refrigerator can help it last even longer, but be mindful to clearly label it—family members might mistake the pulp for something edible, like a strange new spread! Another storage option is the freezer. Frozen papier-mâché pulp keeps for an extended period and, after thawing, can be rejuvenated with the addition of fresh paste and a small amount of water, if necessary.

Preparation

Papier-mâché doesn't need much preparation. You do not need an oven and if you don't intend to form lifesize bears or horses, you don't need a separate studio. However, as papier-mâché is quite sticky, you may want to cover your table with a plastic sheet, which makes the cleaning afterwards very easy. A normal table is completely sufficient. Furthermore, I always use thin protecting latex gloves, because otherwise the printing ink of the newspaper clings persistently to the fingers. At least during the process of producing papier-mâché they are very helpful as otherwise your hands will be black!

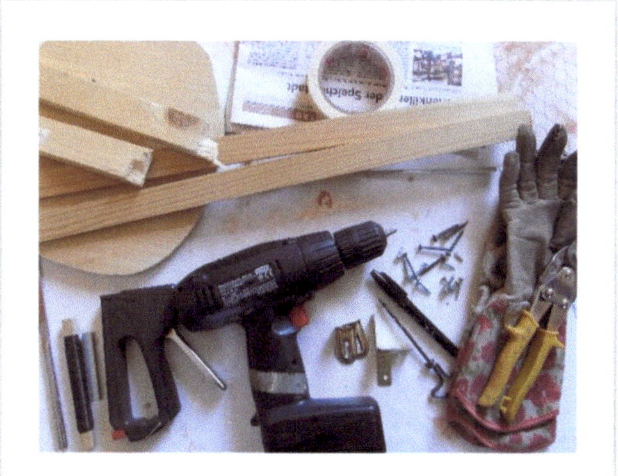

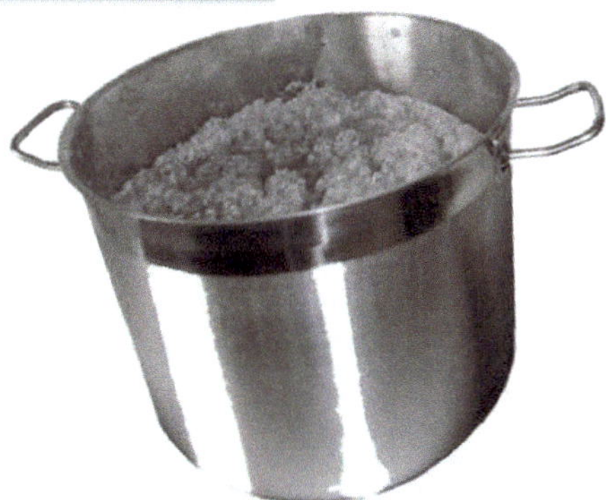

CHAPTER 1

Making ultra-fine papier-mâché

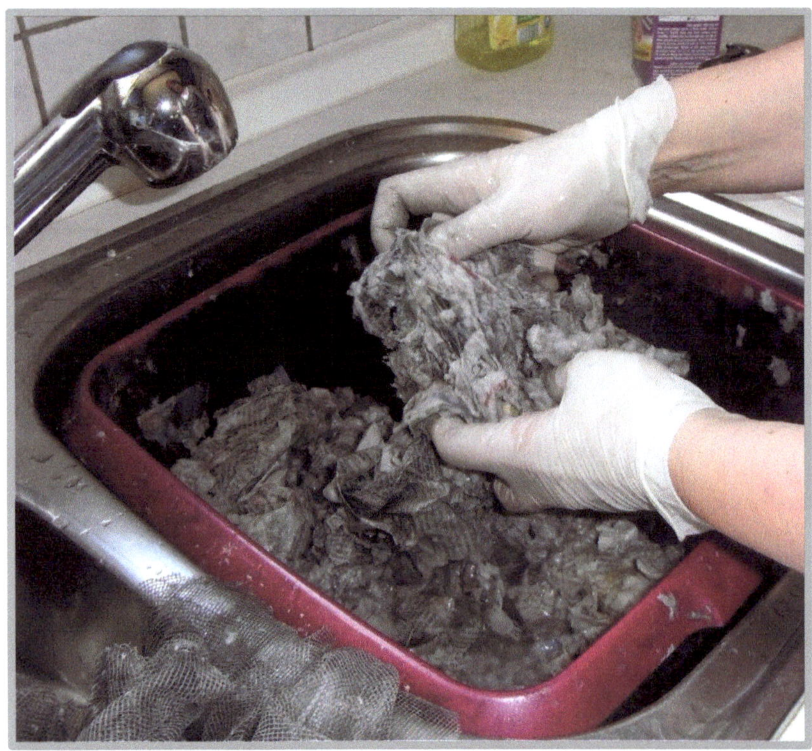

This is what you need for producing papier-mâché

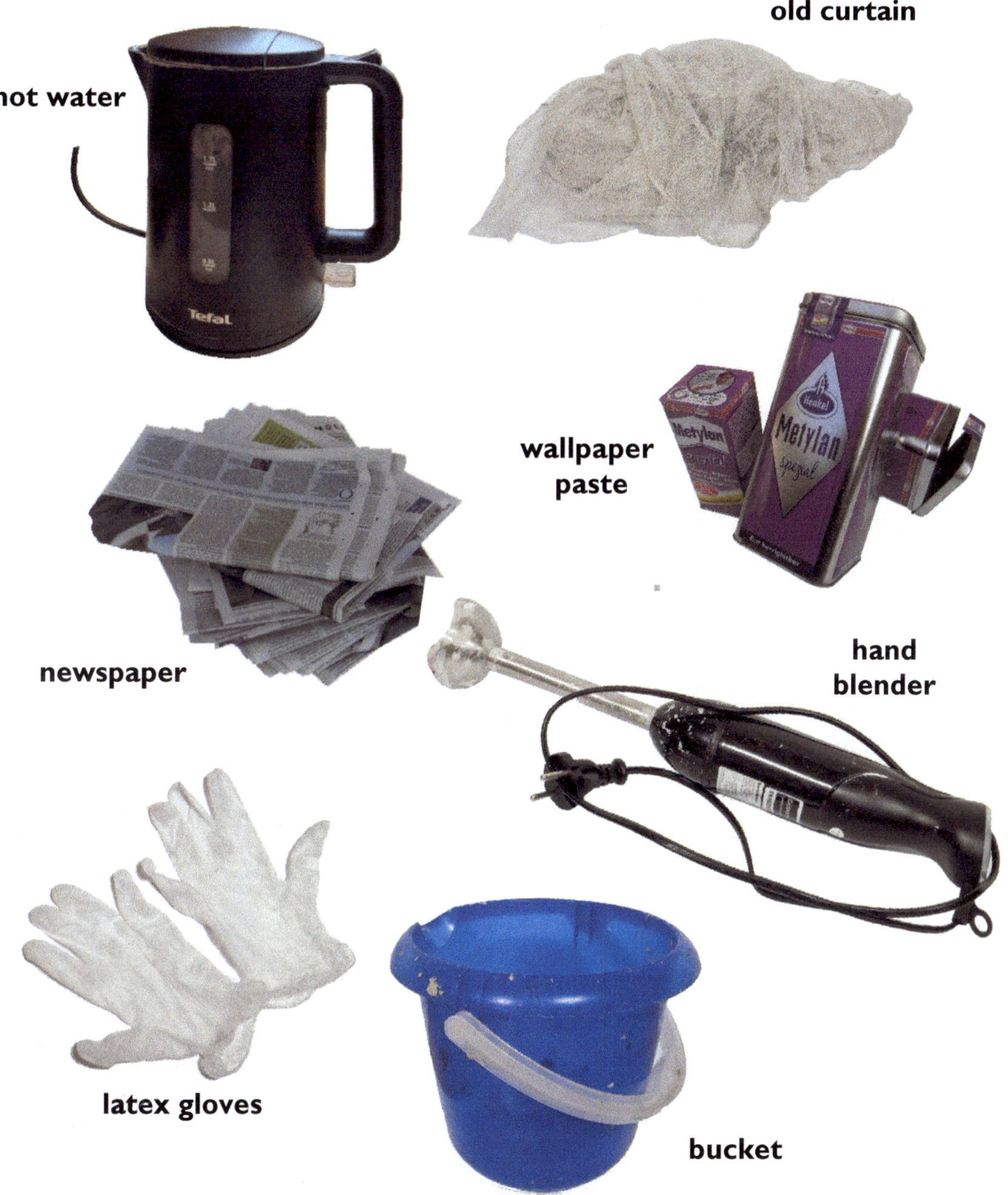

Step by Step – producing papier-mâché

There is more than one way to produce pulp. I tried them all, but at the end of the day I liked my way most. Anyway, it is the most enjoyable way to recycle newspapers.

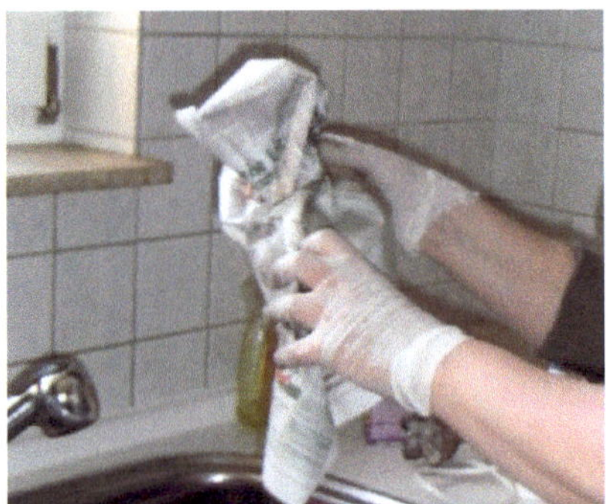

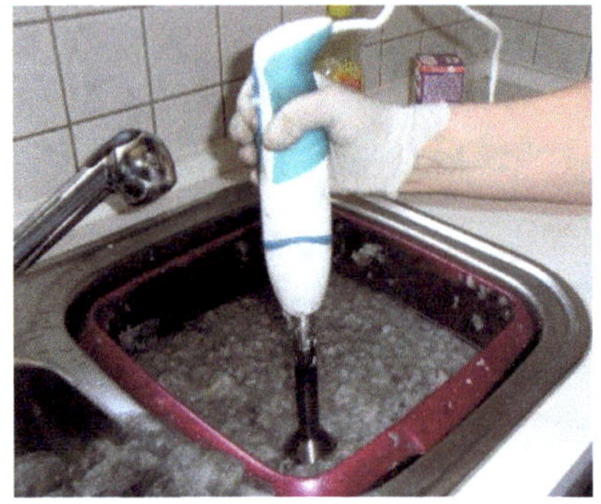

Fill a bucket or a large bowl with hot water – as hot as your hands can endure. Hot water is very good to break up the fibres of the newspaper. Put on your latex gloves. Then fill the bucket with single pages of newspaper. Every 5 - 6 sheets stop adding paper and tear the wet newspapers roughly.

Now take a hand blender and purée the newspapers until you obtain a very smooth grey soup. If you have an old and big pot to sacrifice for papier-mâché you can even boil the whole batch and leave it for a night. Once you have used your pot or your blender for this purpose, you can't use it for food again because of the printing ink. The longer you purée your newspaper soup and the longer it stays in hot water, the finer is the mix.

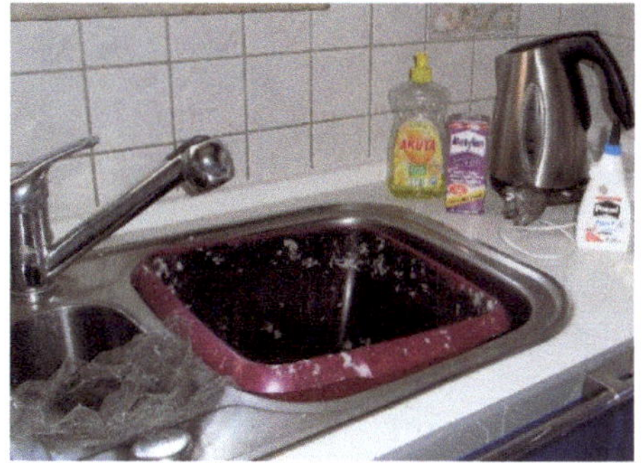

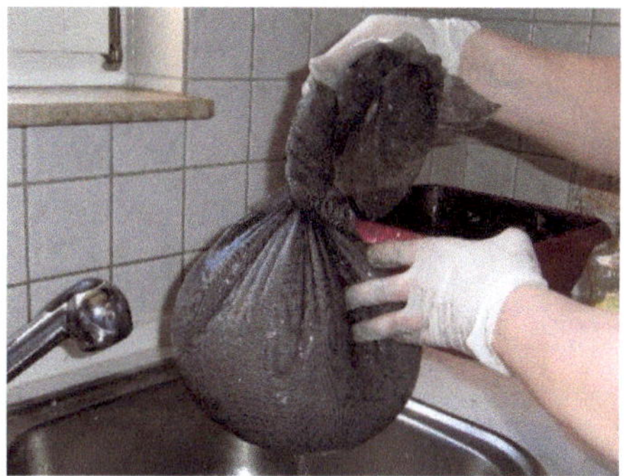

Now lay an old curtain or a fly-screen across your sink and tip the whole bucket of pulp into it. To ensure the curtain stays in place, weigh down the corners with heavy objects like bottles.

Next, take the corners of the net and twist them together to enclose the pulp in a way that does not let any pulp escape. Squeeze the "net bag" until most of the water has been wrung out.

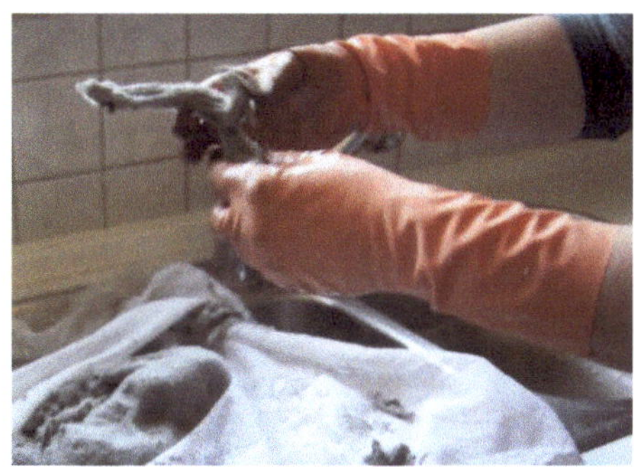

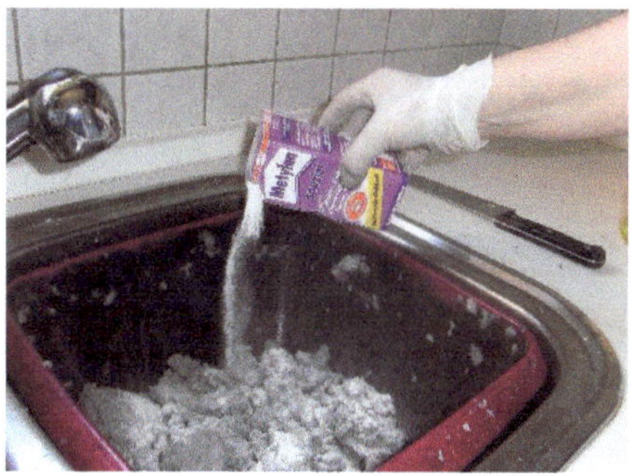

How do you know that you have squeezed your net enough? Open the net and press some of the pulp together. If it doesn't fall apart you have done well. It takes a bit of experience to recognize how wet the pulp has to be. On the one hand moisture is needed to bind the wallpaper paste. On the other hand too much moisture produces a thin pulp, not sticky enough for our purpose. You will soon get a feeling for the right amount of moisture.

In case of doubt squeeze the curtain a bit longer, as it is always easier to add water later, if needed, than to remove it. Now fill the paper purée back into the bucket and add wallpaper paste powder. For about 10 sheets of newspaper you need approximately 4 heaped soup spoons of wallpaper paste powder. Quickly and thoroughly mix it into the pulp, knead it with your hand and leave it for about 10 minutes.

Ready! The pulp is smooth and soft and you can start your project. Some artists add woodglue (1 soup spoon) marble powder (1/2 cup) or clove oil (a few drops).

Woodglue makes the pulp even more stable and helps making your object waterproof.

Marble powder: the pulp will be very hard after drying. You can buy it in an artist store. Disadvantage: it is not easy to cut or sand later.

Clove oil: wards off insects from the drying mass and helps preserve the pulp

We achieve a very smooth pulp by boiling it before adding wallpaper paste. The whole mesh should simmer for a couple of hours after which it should be puréed with a hand blender. Of course this pot should then be reserved for papier-mâché only.

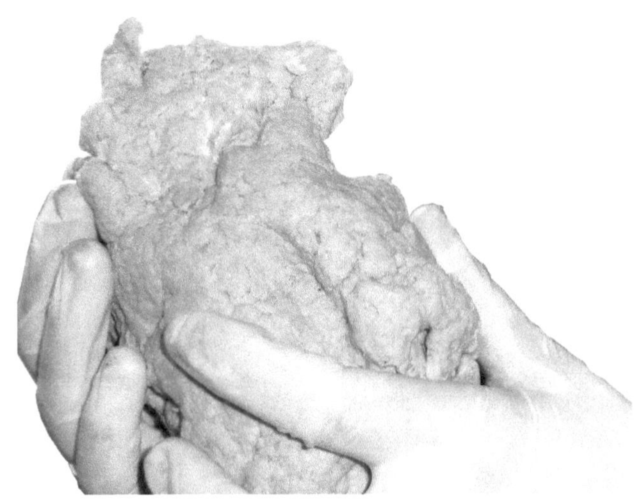

CHAPTER 2

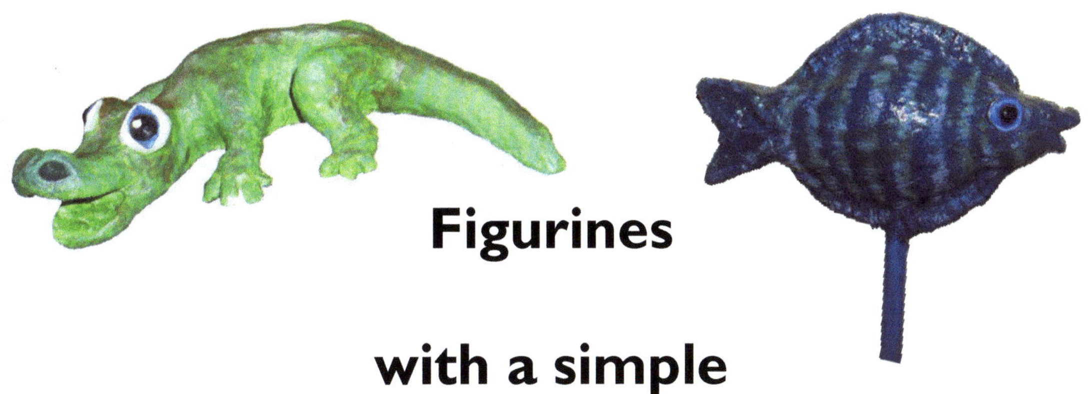

Figurines

with a simple

form

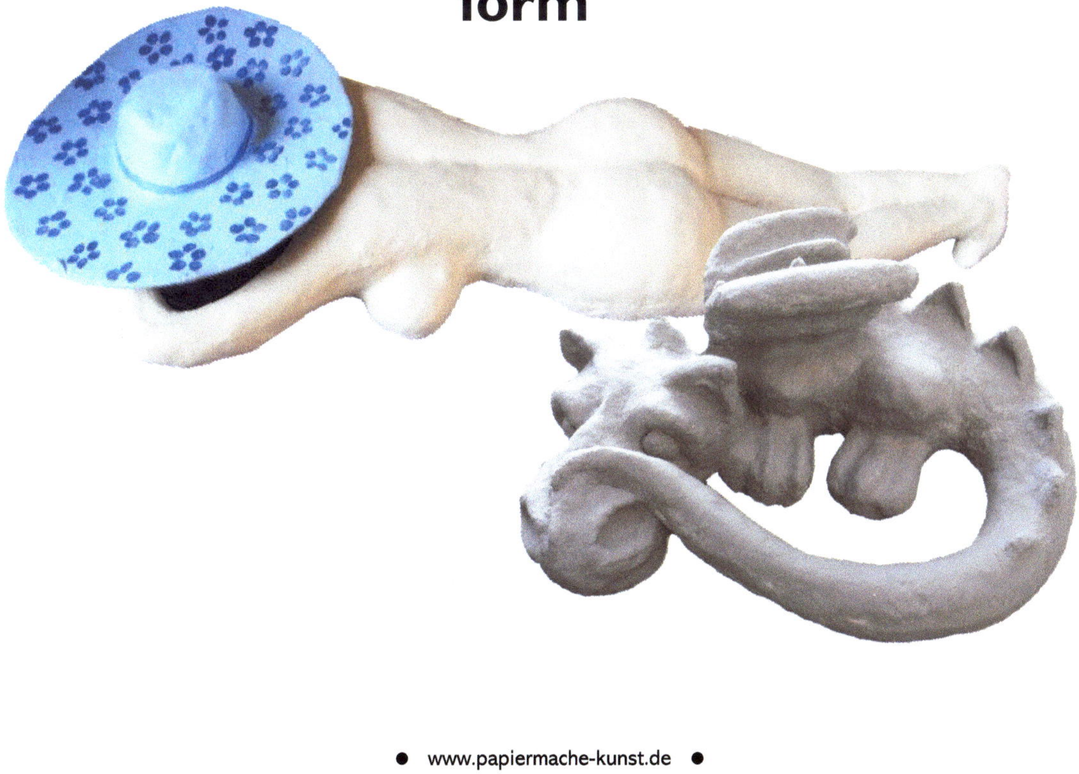

In this chapter I show you how to build a small or flat papier-mâché figurine without too much effort, such as "Nepomuk, the dragon" or "Lying beauty". As both figurines are lying flat they don't need a special solid framework, just newspaper, held in place by masking tape and wire.

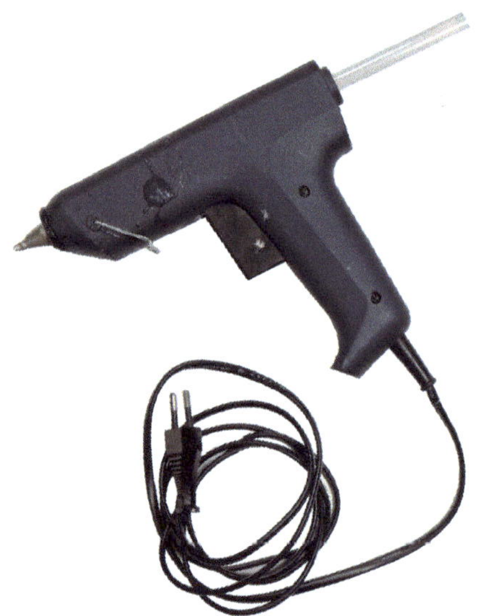

Do you own a hot-melt gun? If not, you should buy one. I think it pays off. And I suggest to buy a good one, for example Bosch hot-melt gun. With the help of a hot-melt you can fix card-board pieces within seconds on your papier-mâché object. It is very stable.

But CAREFUL: The hot-melt must not reach the hands of children and must not be left unattended. The gun reaches a temperature of 200° and even I - with all my precaution - have already suffered from big blisters from burns.

Material

newspaper
masking tape (medium width)
wooden meat skewer
papier-mâché
knifing filler (outdoor)
sandpaper
sealing

Nepomuk,

● the Dragon ●

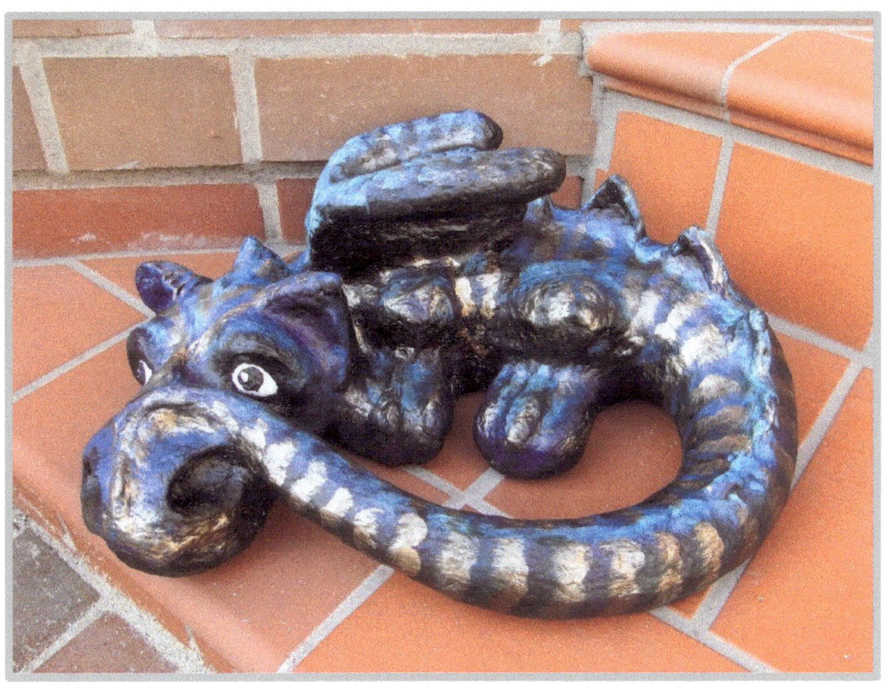

This is what you need for building the dragon:

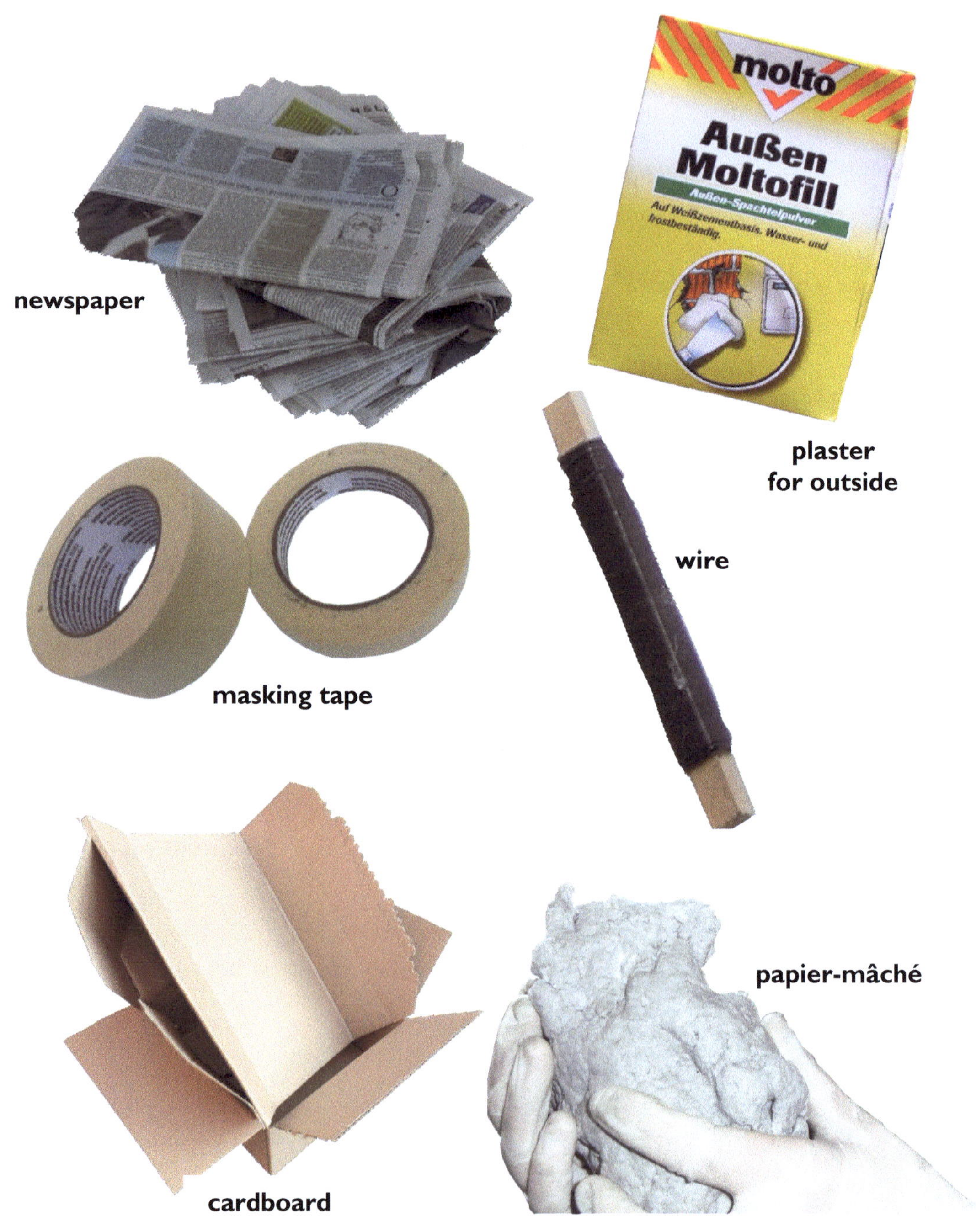

Quite impish Nepomuk looks out from under the tip of his tail. Since our dragon lies flat on the ground he does not need any stabilizing skeleton. However any parts sticking out (like legs or wings) will have to be firmly linked to the body. In the beginning this might take some practising. But you will soon get the hang of it. To illustrate this we will construct the dragon step-by-step which will help to illustrate the technique of forming the structure. This technique may also be applied to other forms of sculptures which have no protruding parts.

Step-by-step

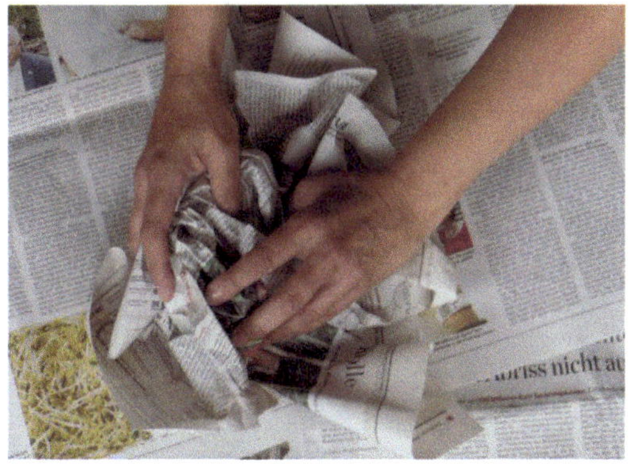

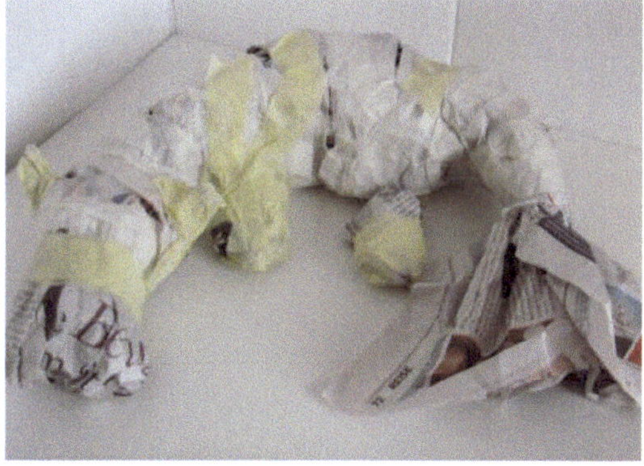

For the inner life we need a structure of tightly squeezed newspapers, pressed into form by masking tape and thin wire.
At the beginning form the body, pressing firmly two sheets of newspaper into a bulgy form.

Squeeze more sheets of paper into form for the neck and the head and fix them with the help of masking tape to the body. Smaller lumps of newspaper can be attached as feet. It is very important that you press the newspaper together very firmly, so that the form doesn't sag when papier-mâché is applied.

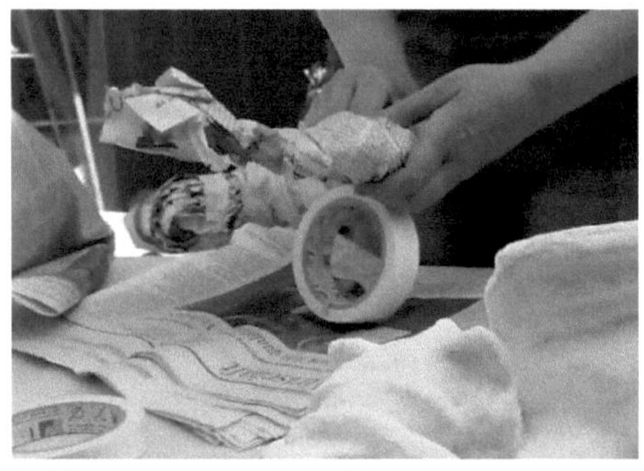

For the tail, create a small shape using newspaper and cover it thoroughly with masking tape. You can wrap wire around the tail for easier shaping later, or attach the tail to the feet using a screw..

Now take your pulp and form mouth, head, eyes, ears, body, feet and tail of the dragon. Let it dry thoroughly. After that fix the tail to the top of the dragon's mouth using hot glue, stapler or adhesive tape.

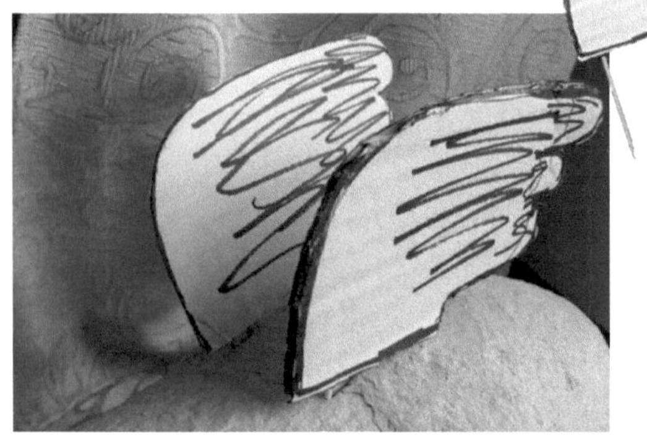

Cut two wings out of stable cardboard. Let them be 1 cm smaller than the final form shall be. Take toothpicks to join body and wings. Stabilize them with hot-melt.

Now cover your dragon completely with Papiermache. Perhaps you want to emphasize the wings by forming individual lines. If you want you can provide body and tail with dorsal fins.

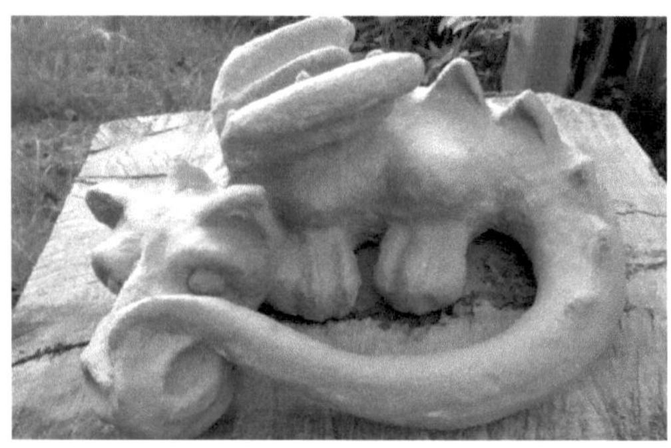

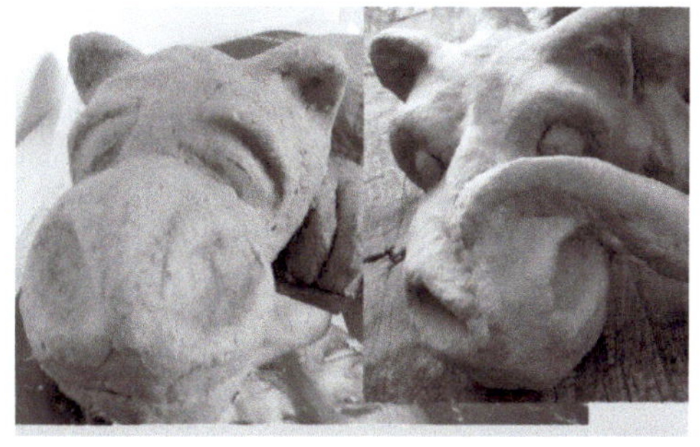

Depending on how you form eyes and nose, the dragon can have a sweet-natured or a hair-raising expression. If I do this dragon it looks different every time.

Leave the bottom side without papier-mâché for the moment. Only when he is dry you can turn your dragon and apply papier-mâché on the bottom side. Flatten the pulp with a knife as if you were spreading butter on bread.

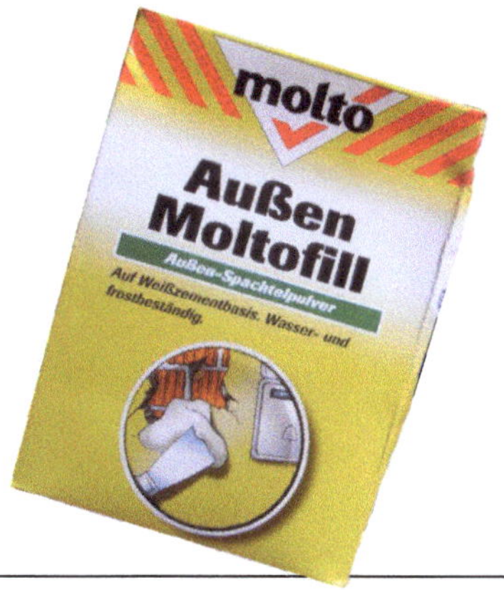

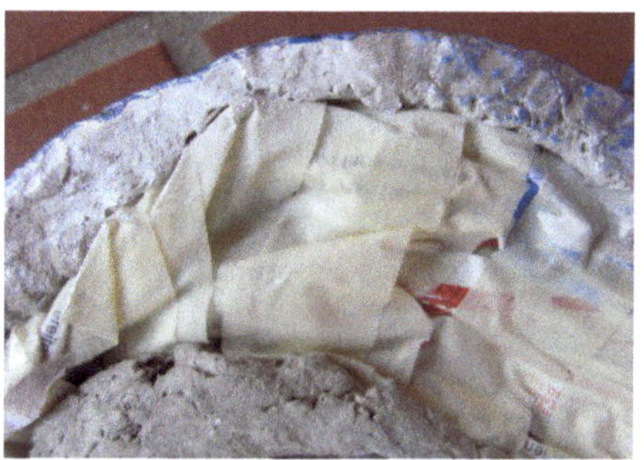

If you want to put your dragon in the garden or if you want to achieve a real smooth surface, you can cover it with a spattling compound like Moltofill (suitable outside). Follow the instructions on the package and brush it on your figure. I will come back later to spattling compounds and fillers.

Sand your figure between two layers of filler until the surface is smooth if you like that. If you want to weatherproof the dragon it is very important that every bit of pulp is covered with waterproof filler.

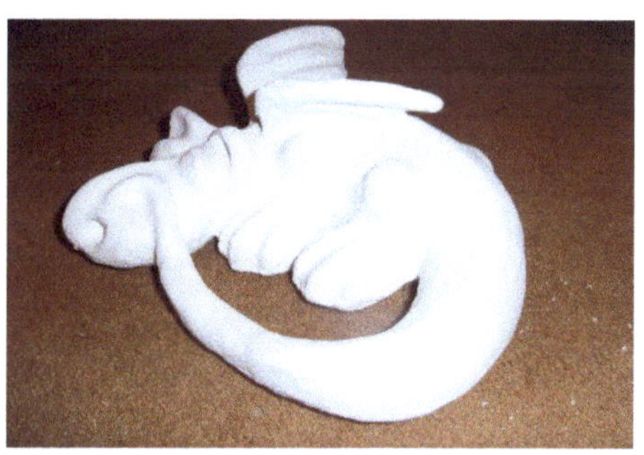

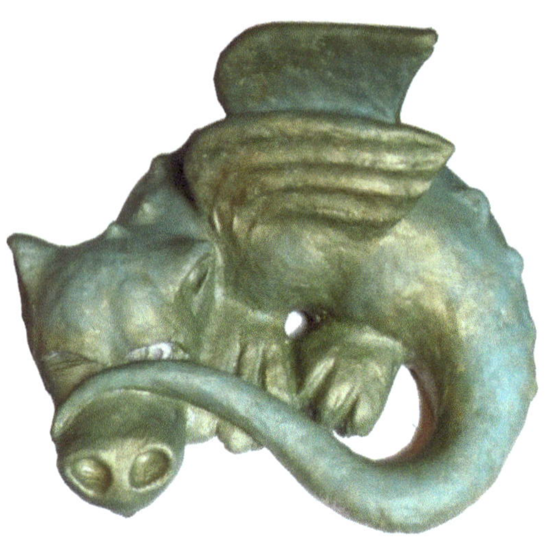

Now cover your dragon with two coats of white varnish for the outdoor area. Then paint it with acrylic colour. After that cover him with varnish for the outdoor area. In order to protect your dragon from moisture of the ground take a cork and cut 4 slices of 1 cm which you fix with a screw to the dragon so that he doesn't touch the ground directly.

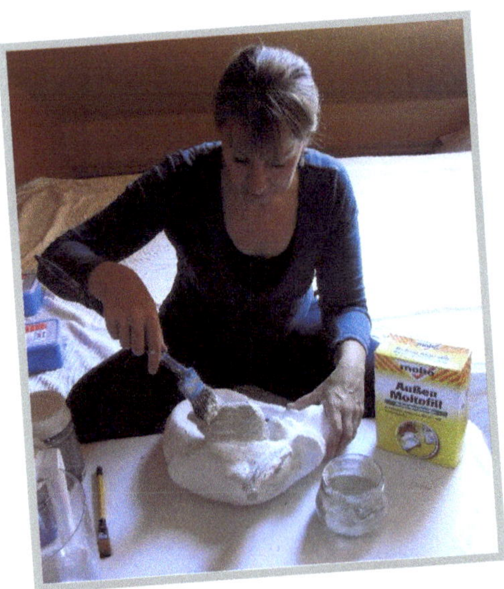

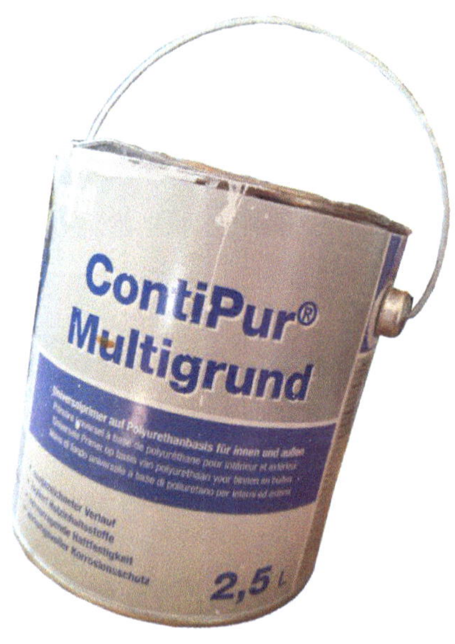

Lying Beauty

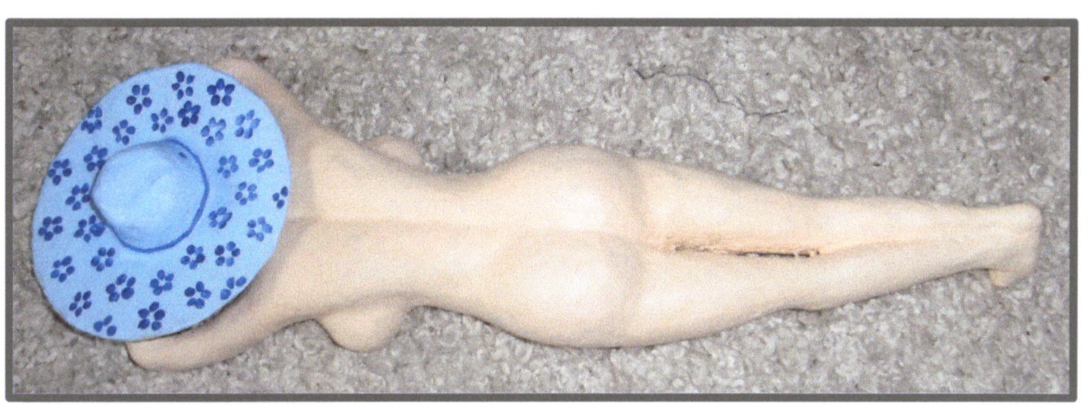

For this tiny form you do not necessarily need an armature of wire, but of course it heightens the stability of this object. And, furthermore, with the help of wire you can bend the arms and legs of the lying beauty as you like them to be. Alternatively you can use sisal reinforced wire, which certainly is quite expensive.

This idea I owe to a workshop participant. She brought a photo of such a figure from her holiday in Greece

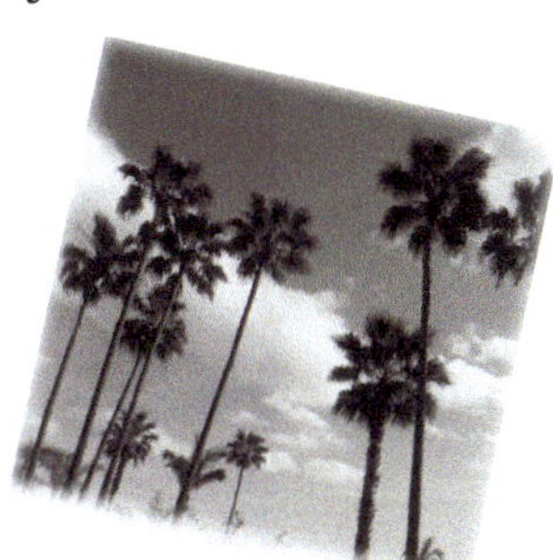

Material
newspaper
masking tape (medium width)
wood glue
cardboard
wire
Master Plate, e.g. CD

Step-by-Step

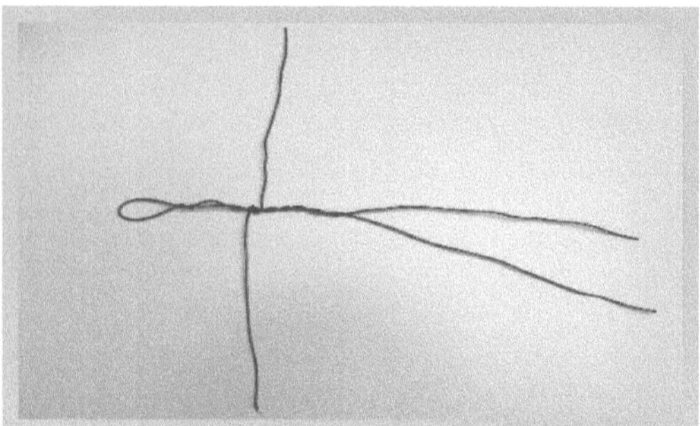

Cut 60 cm piece of wire that you double place, as shown above, and twist a few times in the middle. A loop remains, where the head will be later. Take another wire, 30 cm long, and twist it around the body for shoulder and arms.

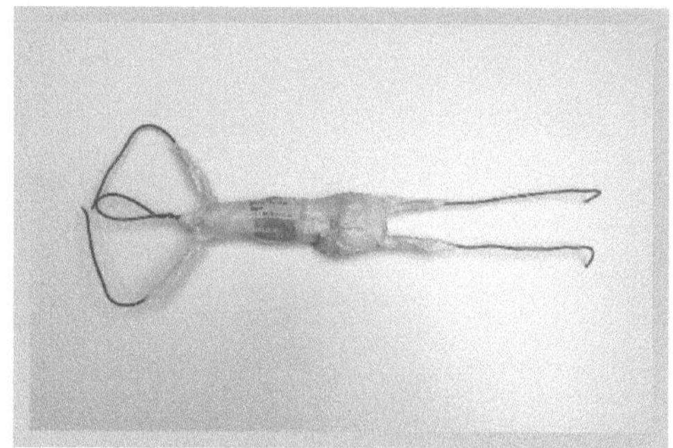

First attach the wire crossing with hot glue or tape on the shoulder. Then wrap a bit of newspaper and tape to the parts of the body which are usually a bit thicker, for example the back, the upper legs a.s.o. Put arms and legs in the desired position

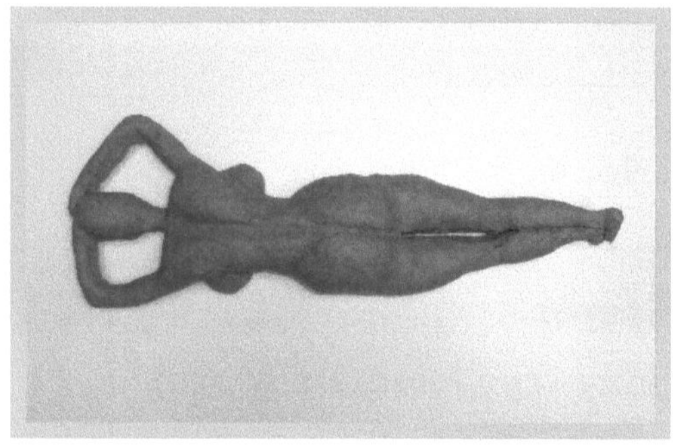

Now you can cover the lying beach beauty with pulp. Depending on your taste the right and left breasts may peep out under the body. You don't have to work very accurately on the head, as the head will be covered by the sunhat later anyway.

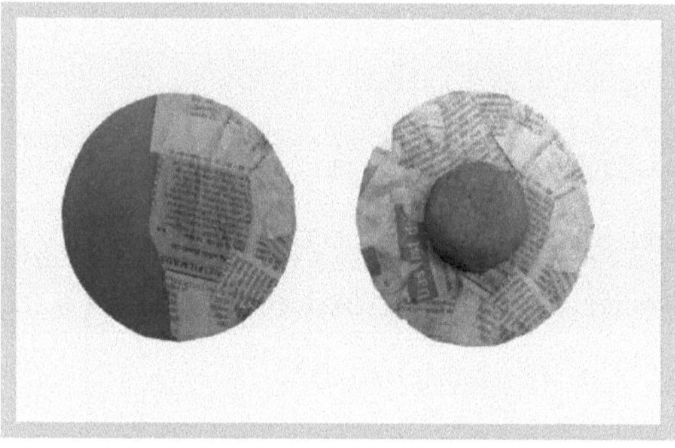

Finally form the sunhat. Well suited is strong cardboard, for example the leftover of a book packaging. You can also use an old CD. Cover the CD with strips of newspaper, so that you can easily paint it later. Complete the hat with a small ball of pulp. Then place the hat on top of the figure.

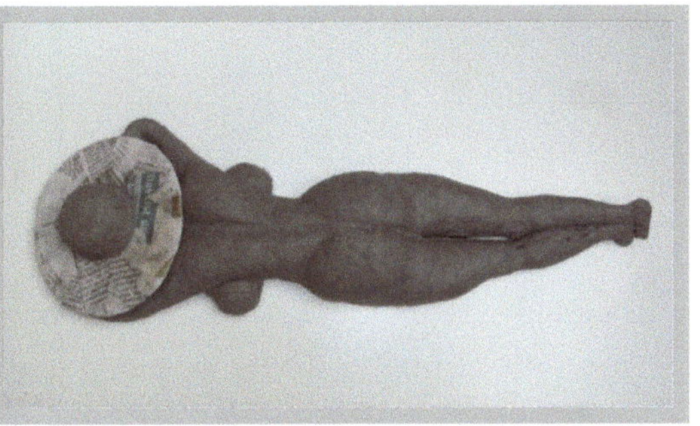

After drying apply a second layer of pulp. This will make the surface a bit smoother. There are some details to look at, for example the backbone and the creases under the bottom. To look at these details will make the figure more real. The legs reduce at the knee and widen at the calves.

Once the figure is dried from above, turn it over and cover the figure from below with pulp.

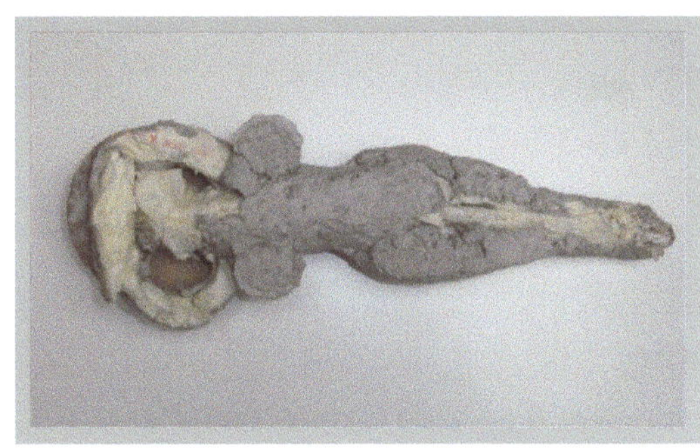

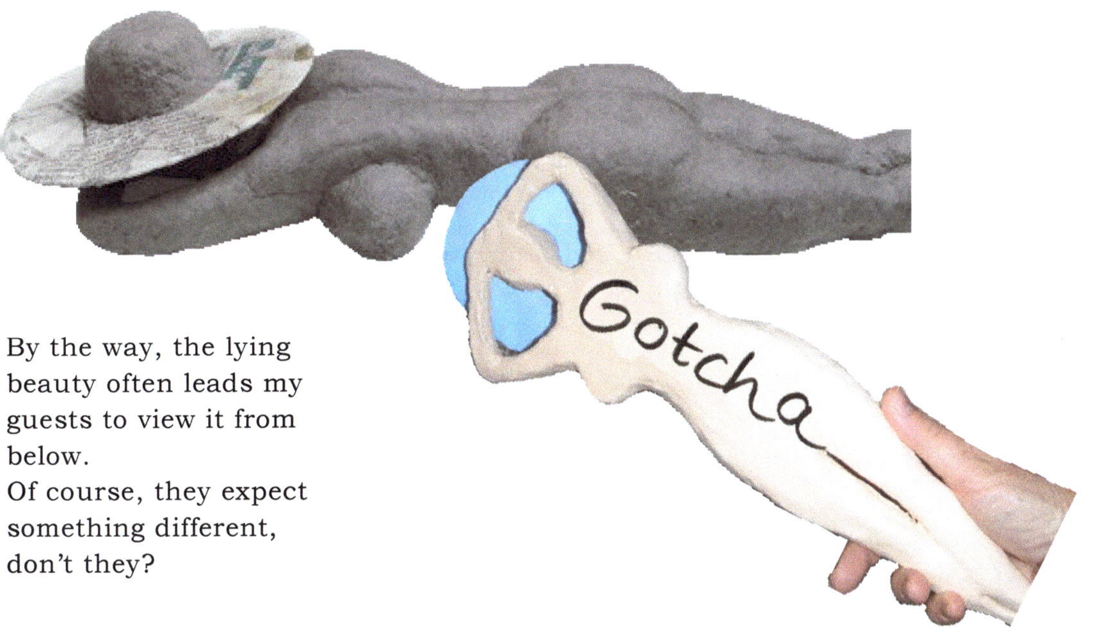

By the way, the lying beauty often leads my guests to view it from below.
Of course, they expect something different, don't they?

Tideland Bird

Cheerful standing sculpture. Easily and quickly formed using 1 ½ Styrofoam balls. Instead of using Styrofoam the basic form may also be constructed by compressing newspaper into the needed balls. However, Styrofoam balls are perfectly shaped and serve well for the start.

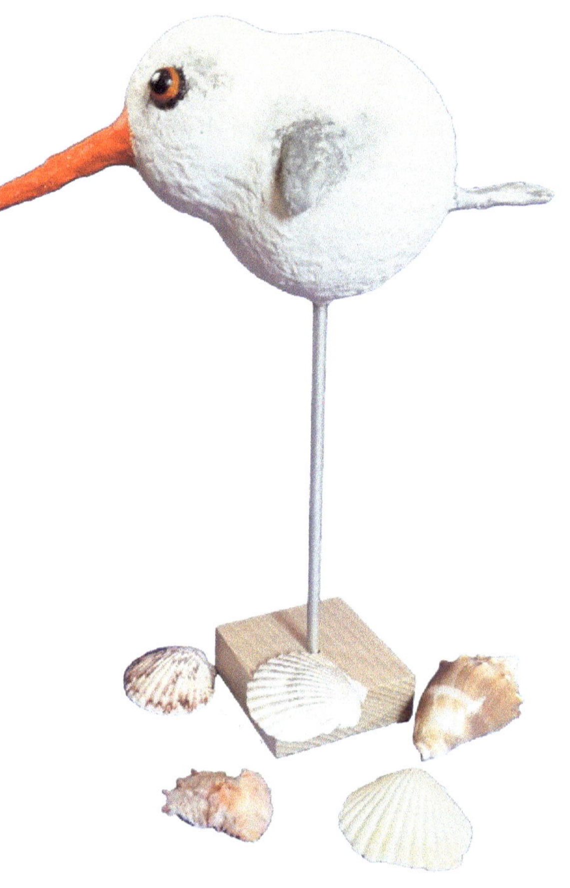

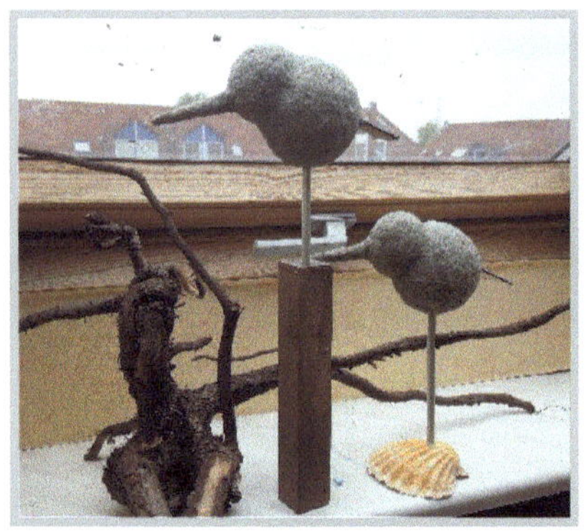

Any sculpture needs a pedestal. For the tideland bird I decided to take a wooden square into which I drilled a hole for an aluminium pole.

Another alternative would be a square made of stone, concrete or even half a shell.

Step-by-step: Tideland Bird

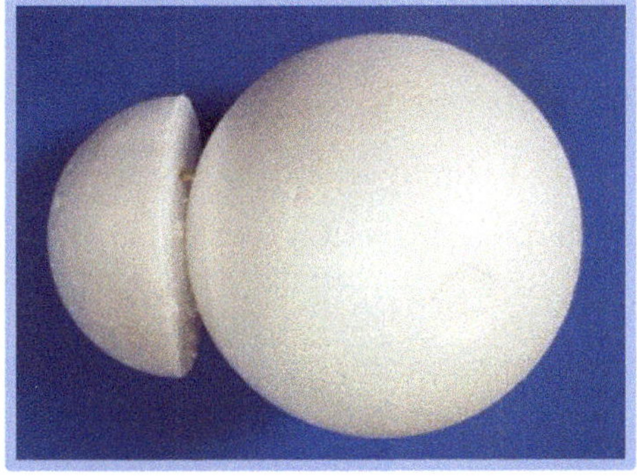

For the figure itself a small and a larger styrofoam ball are needed. The smaller one needs to be cut in half whereas the larger one determines the size of the bird. One half of the small ball is fixed to the body with a wooden meat skewer or tooth pick pressed through the Styrofoam.

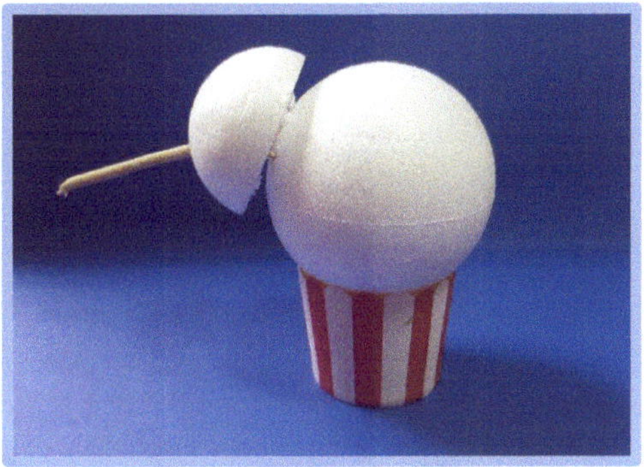

Another meat skewer serves as beak by pressing it through the half of the ball into the large ball. Cut the skew to size with sharp tongs.

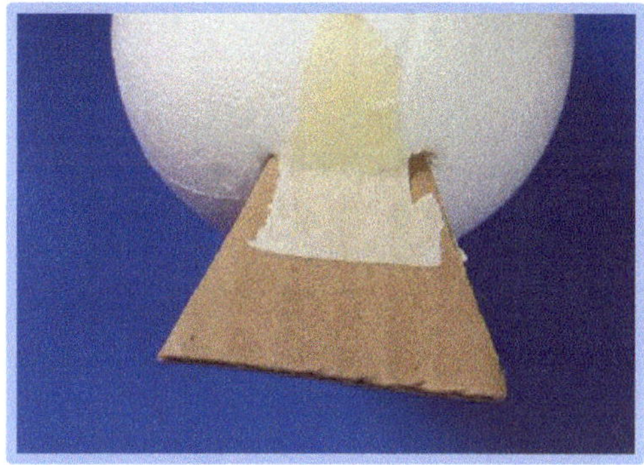

Cut a slot into the lower end of the styrofoam ball and insert a cardboard tail. Fix it with sticky tape.

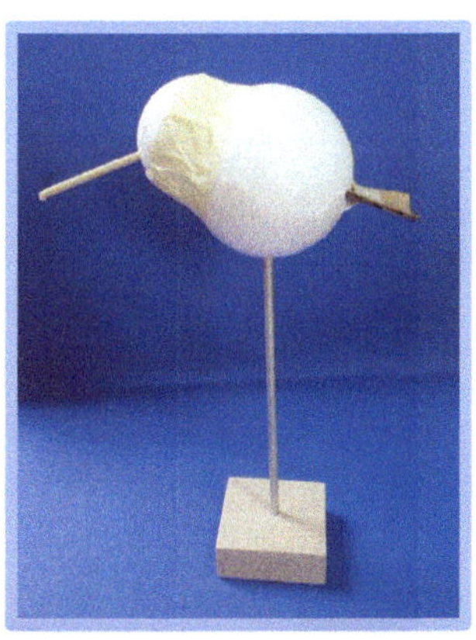

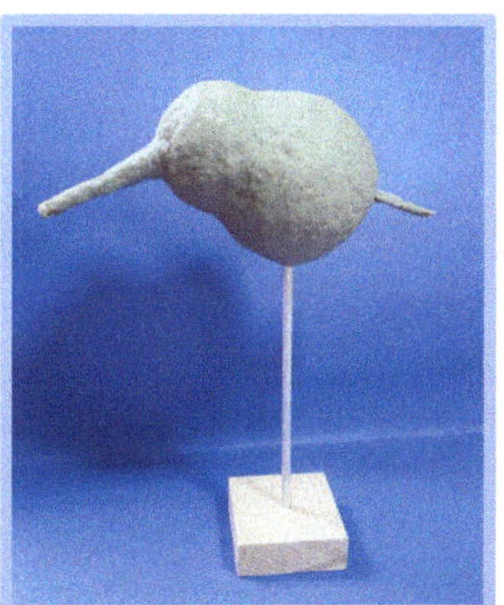

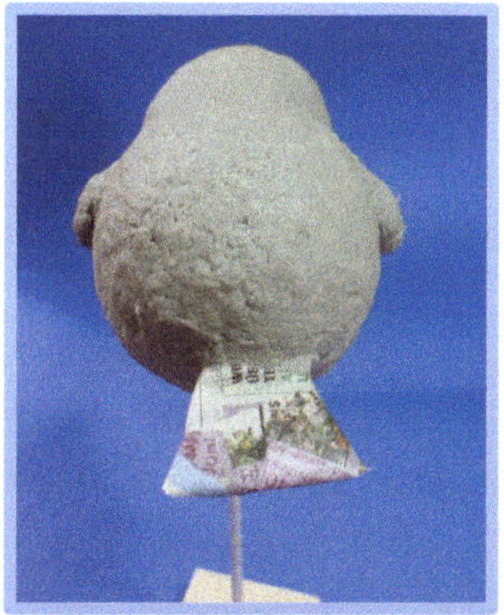

Now press the aluminium pipe into the body. The gap between body and head is closed by masking tape (4) which also stabilizes the head and prevents it from wobbling. And of course we save our precious papier-mâché which would also find it hard to dry in the gap. And now the time has come to apply a thin layer of papier-mâché to form the bird (5). You can prevent the typical bumps from occurring by finally spreading the material with a knife or stroke the surface with wet gluey fingers. The cardboard of the tail will be laminated (6) with newspaper snippets glued onto it, keeping it nice and flat.

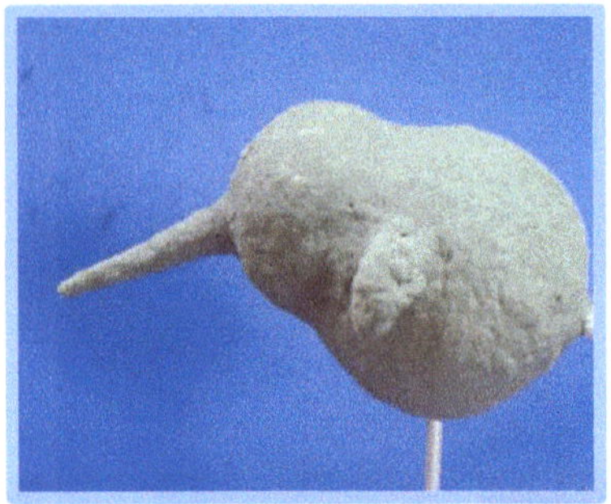

If you like you may also form little winglets at this point. Leave the whole figure to dry thoroughly before applying paint.

The eyes may either painted directly onto the sides of the head or you cut very small Styrofoam balls in half and glue them onto the head – which you then paint. Don't forget the "light spot", it will give a more lively impression.

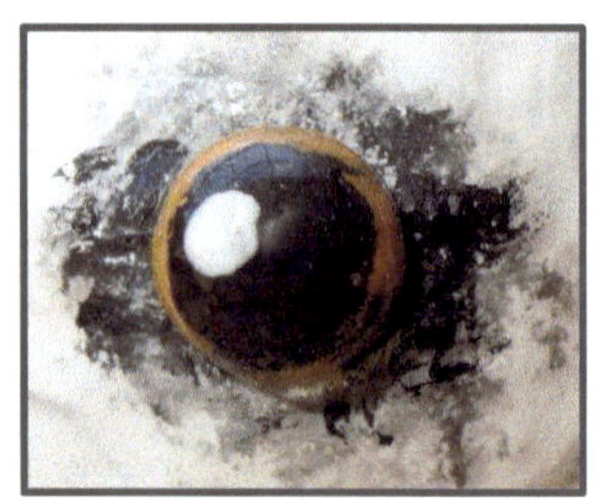

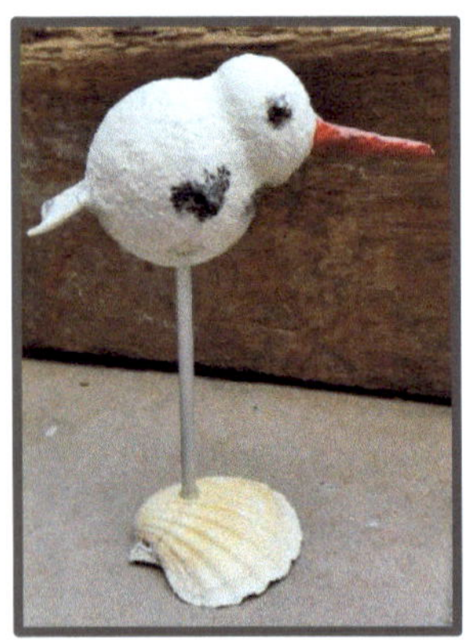

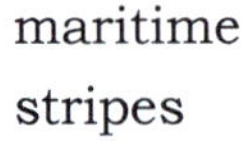

When painting the little fella it is sufficient to use wallpaint directly applied onto the body.
If you like give him a maritime look by painting stripes

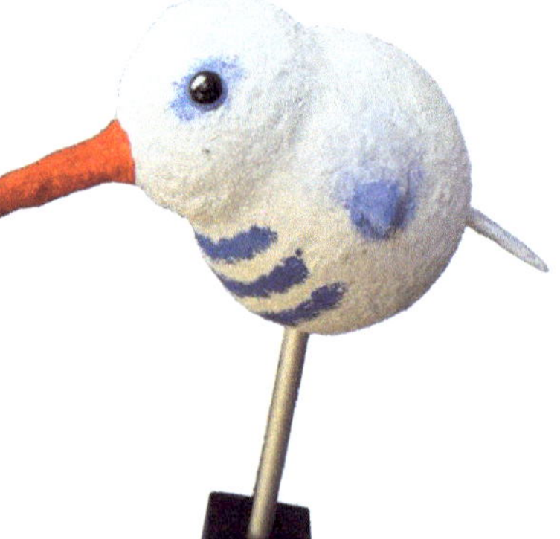

CHAPTER 3

Creating hollow forms with balloons

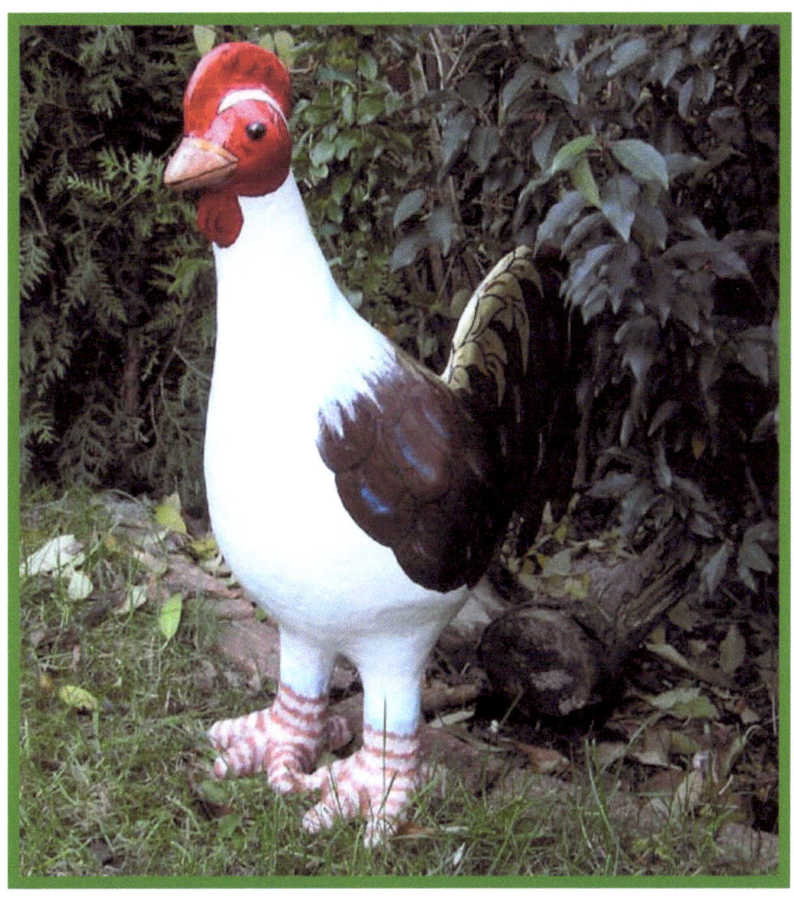

This is what you need for the rooster

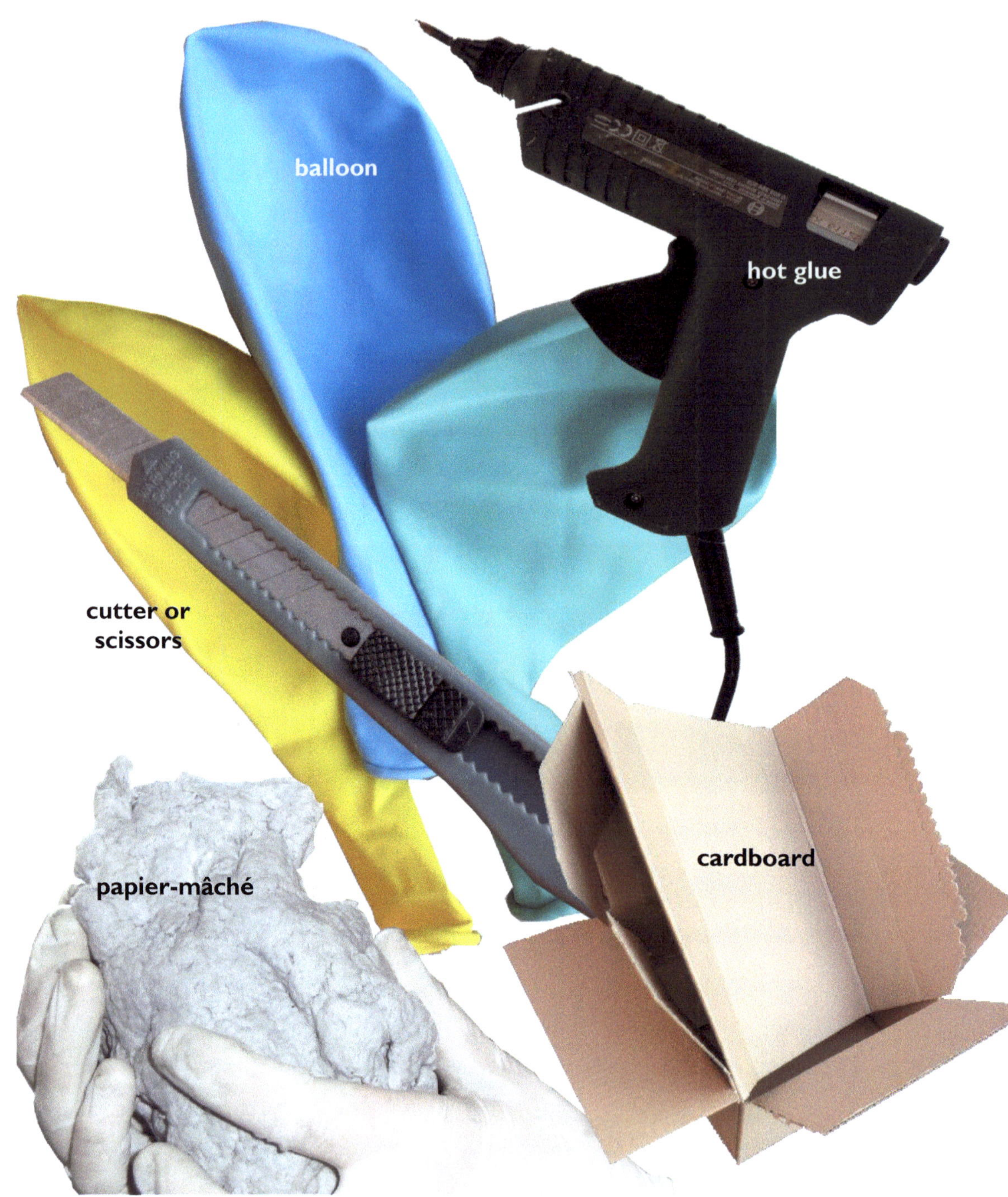

Small Excursion: the masking method

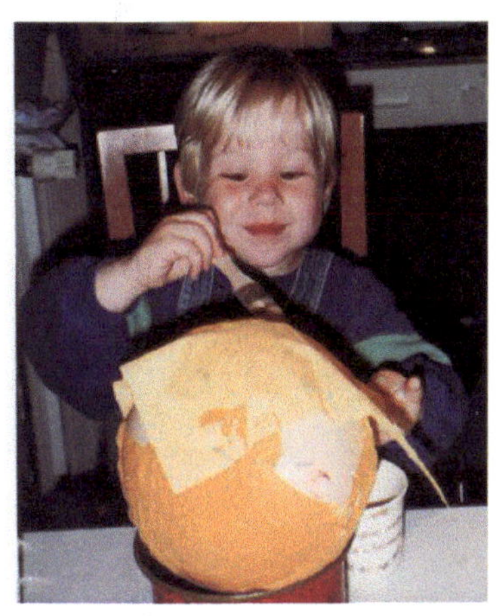

I want to share this method with you. In Kindergardens and schools children form all sorts of objects which have to be hollow, such as piggy banks, pinjatas or vases. This method is ideal when hollow objects have to be illuminated from the inside, for example light-stones, lampshades and many more. Sometimes this technique is referred to as papier-mâché. However, this term is not entirely accurate, as the word papier-mâché originates from the French term, which translates to 'chewed paper', referring to the process of creating a pulp-like mixture from shredded paper. For the masking method, you will cover a substructure like a balloon with small snippets of paper. It is essential to apply several layers to achieve the desired thickness. While this method is less stable than a solid form built using paper pulp, it has the significant advantage of drying much faster. However, it requires careful handling. A hollow and dried structure can soften if you later apply pulp, for example, when adding features like shoulders or a neck.

I often rely on this technique when creating thin or lightweight components, such as "Nepomuk's" wings.

Tip: Use a different color for each layer of paper. This allows you to easily track how many layers you've applied, reducing the risk of missing areas or uneven thickness.

When creating delicate wings for a bird
or a dragon I laminate a layout of several
meat skewers with some layers of thin
paper (eg. tissuepaper, soft tissue or
newspaper). Those wings should always be
manifactured separately and fitted as one
of the last steps. Although these wings are

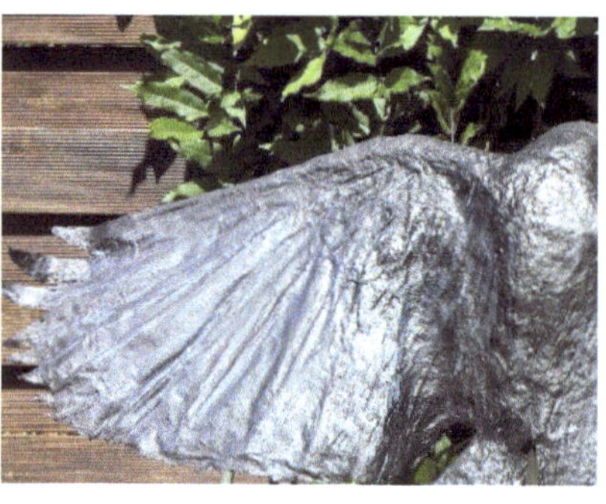

relatively stable, they might be damaged when working on the sculpture.
Also for moulding "clothes" I use this technique
to fold and glue thin layers of newspaper or soft
tissue to form collars, plaits, folds etc. It is
quite easy to align them with an edge or curve.
Combine both methods if you like. On the
Figure (right picture) I formed most parts of
papiermache, but the collar by applying the
masking method.

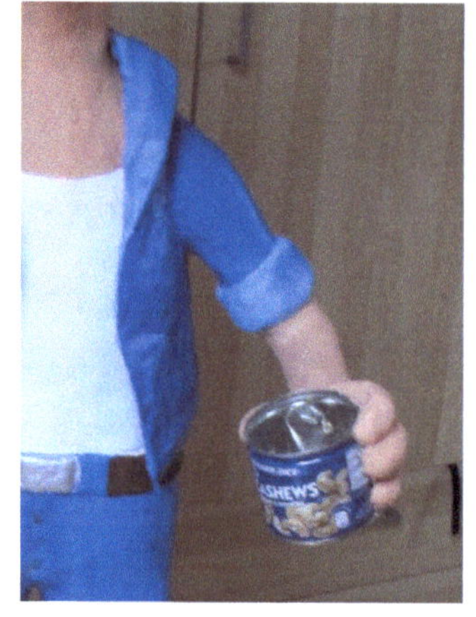

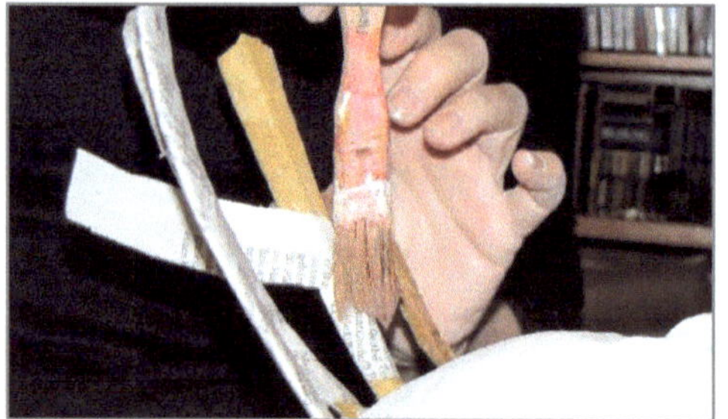

Apart from
these examples I mostly work with pulp,
because I value the robust almost wood-
like consistency when it has dried off
completely. Producing a piece of art quite
frequently is a process in which
approaches as well

as designs change in the course of emergence. It happened that I decided to
cut off parts or wanted to screw other parts onto the sculpture. This of
course would have been impossible with a hollow ball laminated on a
balloon.

Step-by-Step: the proud rooster

For this rooster and all other figures presented here I did not form the basic shape with the masking method but with pulp. Thus, the hollow figure receives a very high stability which is important if you want to use it as a basic form for further processing. Of course, you cannot use this stable forms for lanterns and pinatas, since the mold is covered with massive pulp and therefore not

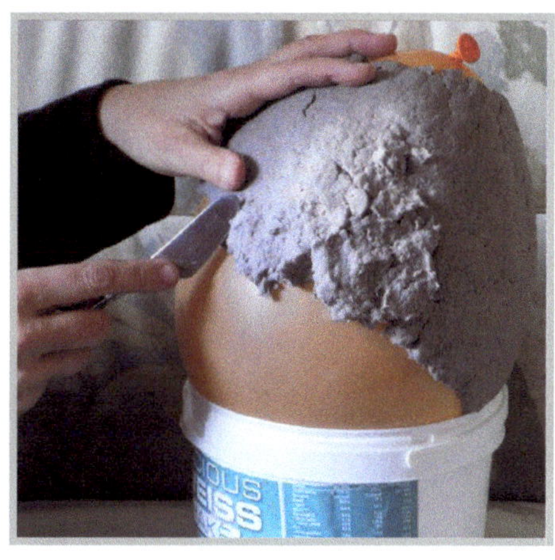

longer transparent and it cannot be illuminated from inside (lantern). On the other hand you can do further work on them, such as adding legs, nose or ears.

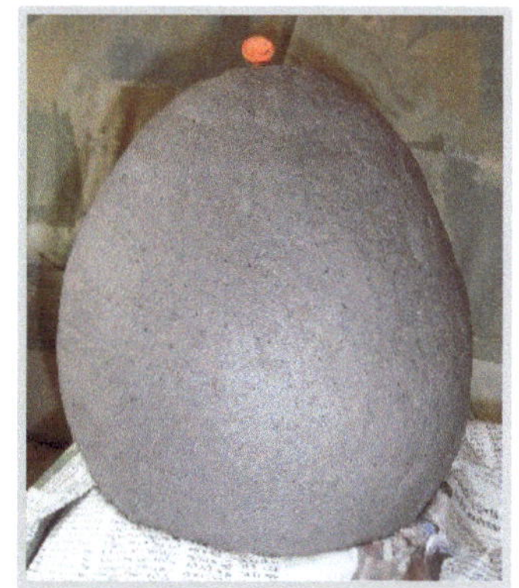

First, fill a balloon with air until it reaches the desired size and until it feels tight enough. If the balloon stays wobbly, it is difficult to apply pulp on it. Blow up the balloon to its full capacity. If you prefer a smaller form, please take a smaller balloon, instead of only blowing it up to half the size.

Now cover the entire balloon with a thin layer of papiermache, approximately 0,5 inch . Please make sure that the papiermache is sticky enough and contains high-quality wall-paper paste. If the consistency of the pulp is not right, the material gets crackings and does not stick to the balloon.

Allow the form to dry completely – this process can take at least a week. To do this, place the balloon, now covered with papier-mâché pulp, on a pot or another stable surface to keep it steady and prevent it from tipping over.

After a few days, gently turn the balloon so that the part resting on the pot is now on top, allowing it to dry evenly all around.

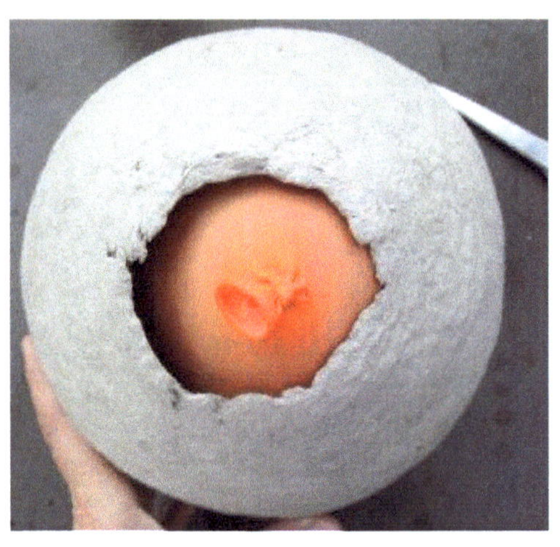

To check if the form is fully dry and hardened, press lightly on the sides of the balloon. If the surface feels firm and doesn't give under gentle pressure, the papier-mâché is ready for the next step. Patience pays off! A thoroughly dried papier-mâché form will be more durable and sturdy.

As the balloon gradually loses air and starts to shrivel, you'll notice it naturally pulling away from the dry papier-mâché shell. This separation is a good indicator that the form is ready for the next step.

Once the papier-mâché is completely dry and sturdy, take a thin needle and carefully pop the balloon. At this point, the balloon is no longer needed. The hollow papier-mâché shell that remains will serve as the body of your rooster or hen.

If you plan to create a piggy bank instead, remember to leave a small opening during the crafting process to remove the balloon's remains and to provide a slot for depositing coins. However, don't worry if the rubber stays inside—it won't affect the final product.

Use sturdy cardboard, such as material from a delivery package, to create the tail, beak, and feet of your figure. Cut these shapes based on the drawing provided as a guide. Keep in mind that the drawing is just a suggestion—feel free to adjust the designs to your liking or the character you're building. For the legs, you'll need durable cardboard tubes. The inner tubes from cling film or aluminum foil rolls work well, as they are much stronger than

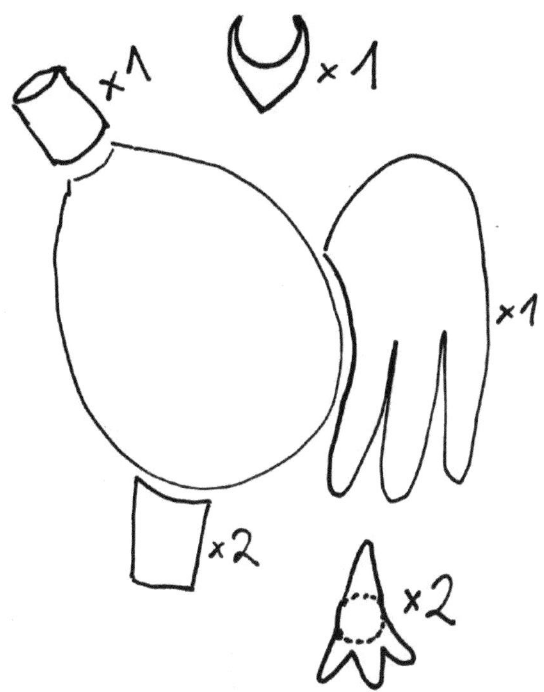

those from toilet paper rolls. Cut two sections approximately 5–10 cm long for the legs. These will provide stability to your figure. For the neck, opt for a slightly wider cardboard tube, such as the inside roll from a kitchen paper towel. This will give the neck the right proportion compared to the body and legs. Before attaching the parts, it's important to adapt their shapes to fit the curved body. Trim the edges as needed so they contour smoothly to the surface of the papier-mâché ball. Ensure the lower ends of the legs are flat and level, as they will rest directly on the surface your figure stands on. When all the parts are ready, use hot glue to securely attach them to the body. If you don't have a hot glue gun, a strong all-purpose glue will also work, though it may take longer to set. Be sure to align all the pieces properly before the glue dries, and give everything ample time to cure for a sturdy and stable structure.

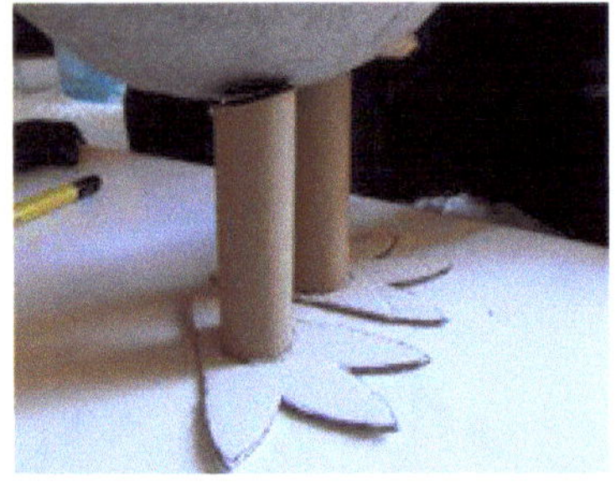

The next step is to stuff the legs with a small piece of newspaper, so that the tubes stay firm and solid, even if they get wet by layers of papier-mâché. Then glue the legs to the body. Small gaps can be closed with hot glue.

The cardboard beak should be shaped according to the tube. You can use the tube as a template for the shape.

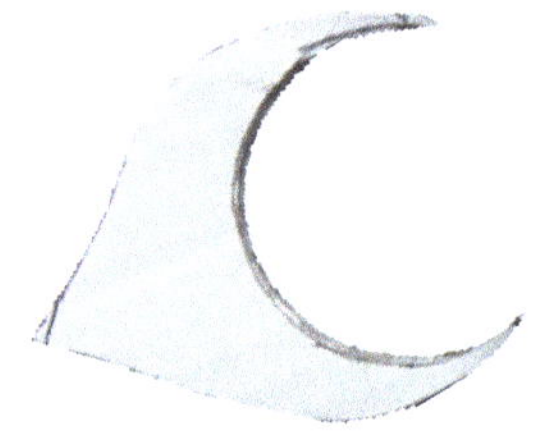

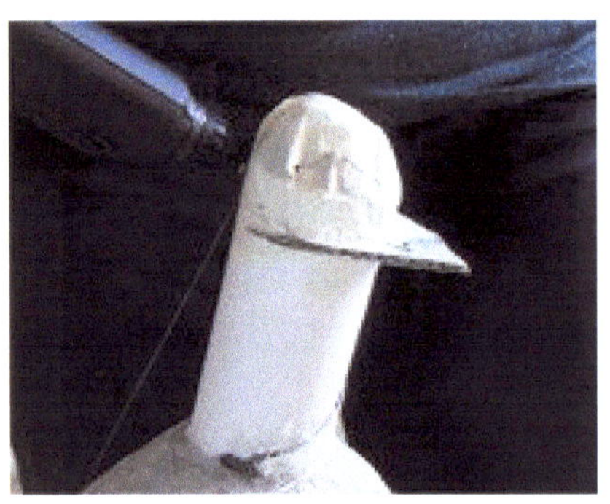

Now you can easily attach the beak with hot glue on the neck. Fill the neck with small newspapier pieces and leave a little ball of newspaper to form the upper part of the head. Attach it with masking tape to the neck.

For the tail you need solid cardboard, so that it won't bend when covered with papier-mâché . Cut out a form according to the picture and fix the tail with hot glue to the body. Here is your rooster. If you choose to make a hen you do not need a cardboard tail (see suggestions a little later)

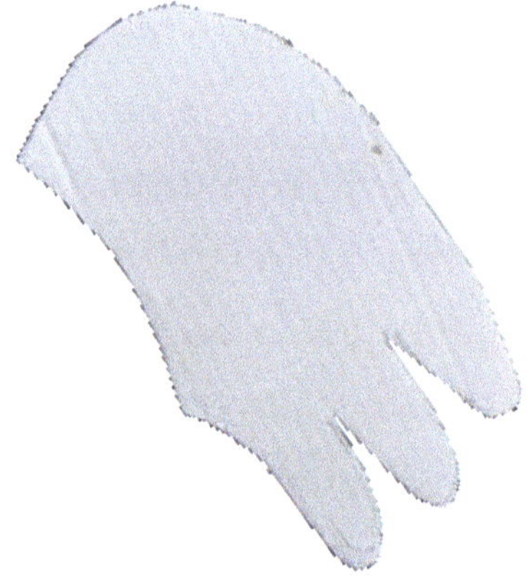

Take a bit of pulp and spread it everywhere where cardboard tubes or pieces meet the pulp ball. That helps to build stability.

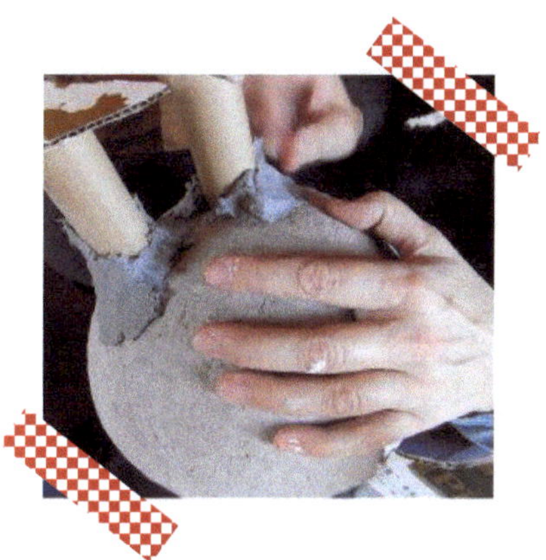

Ensure that the rooster is well-balanced when attaching the legs and feet. If it leans forward or backward, this is often due to wet or damp papier-mâché, which is naturally heavier than the dry, hardened material and tends to pull downward. To prevent this imbalance, it's a good idea to work on both sides alternately, applying material evenly to maintain symmetry and stability throughout the construction process. To keep the tail lightweight and avoid unnecessary strain on the structure, you might consider using a laminating technique. This involves layering thin sheets or strips of papier-mâché instead of adding bulky, heavy pieces. By doing so, you can create a detailed and sturdy tail without adding too much weight, ensuring the final piece is stable and well-proportioned.

For the claws you need small lumps of pulp about the size of a walnut. They may be modelled rather like comicbook characters: a little plumpish and foolish. Which would of course also help to give it a good stand. Then start modelling head and beak, followed by

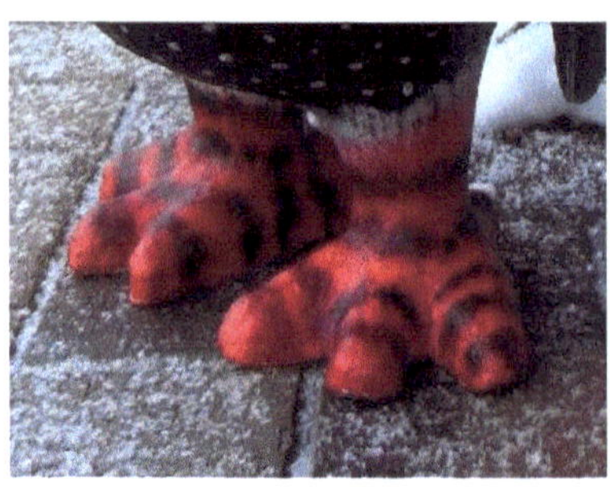

covering the sculpture with Papier-mâché . Form thickenings where cardboard parts and body join, eg. thigh, throat, tail and beak.

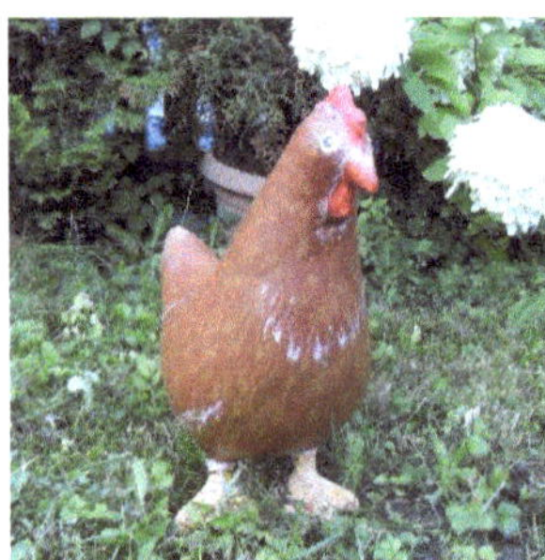
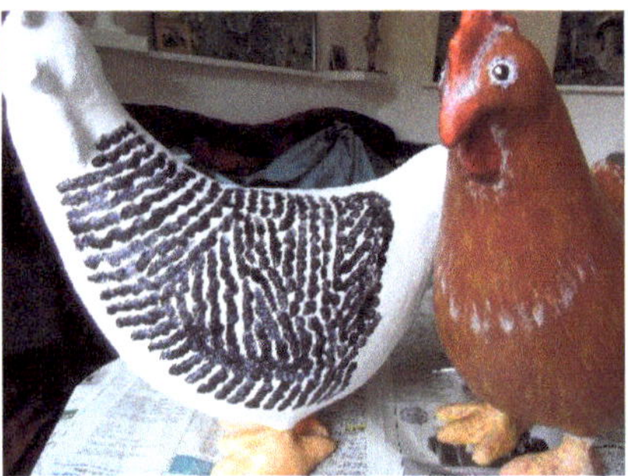
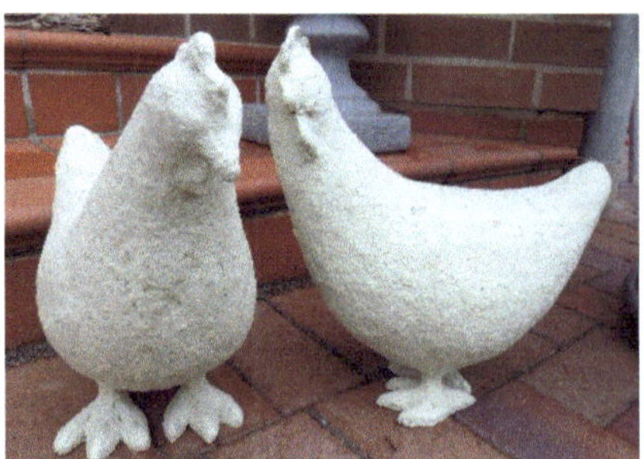

Painting:

If you want to place the rooster/the chicken outside on the terrace I suggest you cover the whole sculpture with knifing filler or spattling compound. Best finish up with two layers of acrylic paint. The feather optic is best accomplished by stroking a nearly dry paint brush with a small amount of colour smoothly over the now painted surface – as shown at the models above. This will show a light featherlike effect.

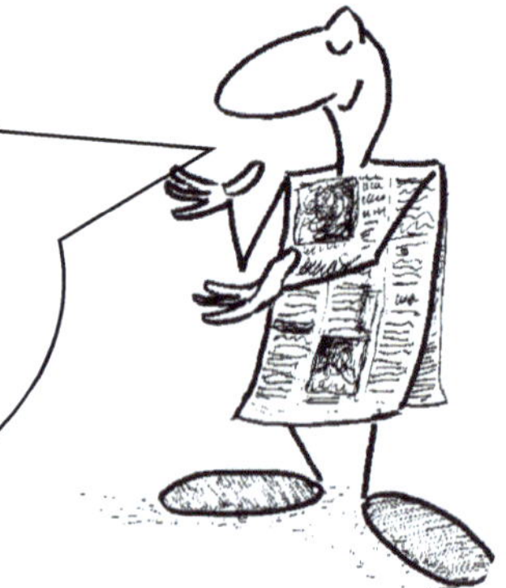

The teacup-table

Attention: for this furniture highlight you need patience and a lot of Papier-mâché. Papier-mâché shrinks by approx. 5% when it dries. When the water in the mixture has evaporated, the surface remains slightly bumpy. The thicker the layer, the more noticeable this is. That's why I usually work with two layers. I just let the first layer shrink and allow it to dry. Then I set to work on a very fine (more preparation-intensive) layer of pulp that has been mixed for a little longer. Especially for objects that need a lot of material – like this teacup-table – I create the raw form with normal Papier-mâché and take my extra-fine Papier-mâché only for the last layer.

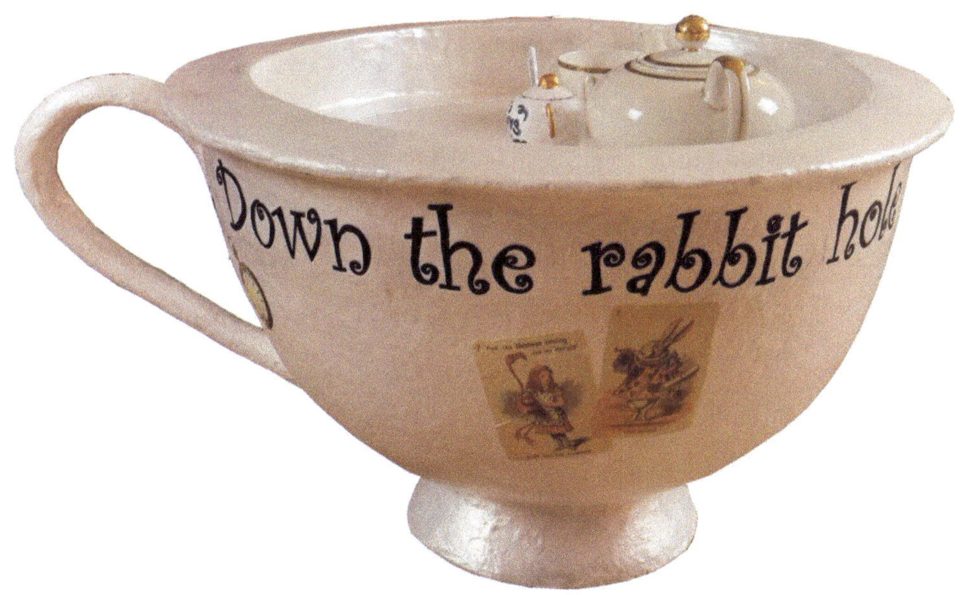

Step-by-step: the teacup table

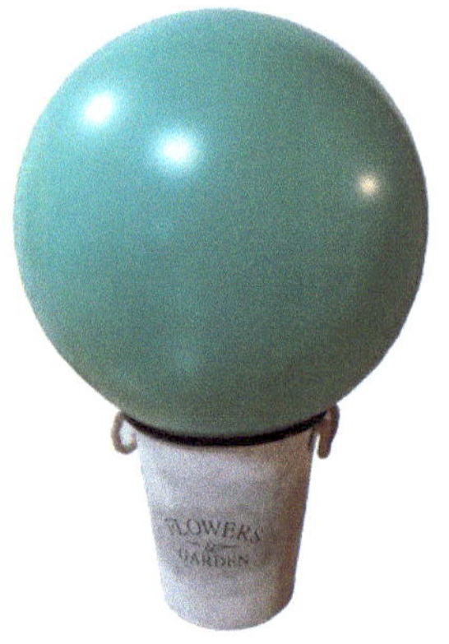

For the initial shape, inflate a large balloon. The diameter of the balloon when inflated corresponds to the diameter of the teacup table. Do not inflate the balloon to the maximum so that it does not burst, but it must not be too soft either, because otherwise it would deform too much under the weight of the papermache layer. It is best to rest the balloon in a large bucket. Because of the pulp, it quickly becomes too heavy and might then tip over.

First, brush a relatively thin layer of paper mache on the balloon. The mixture should not be applied thicker than 0.5 inch. Otherwise, it could cause the layer to slip down the balloon, or worse, cause the balloon to deform like an egg due to the weight.

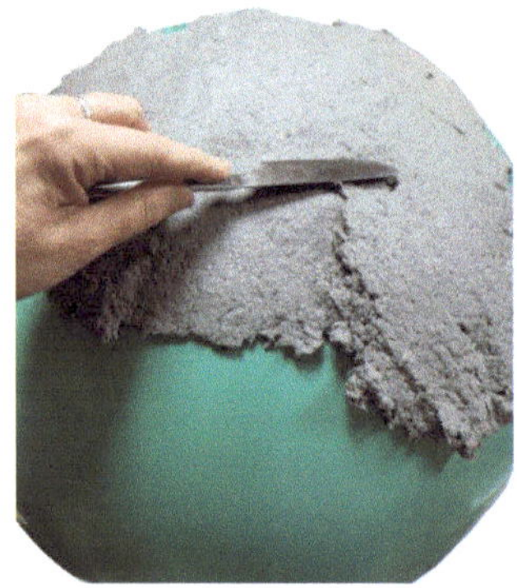

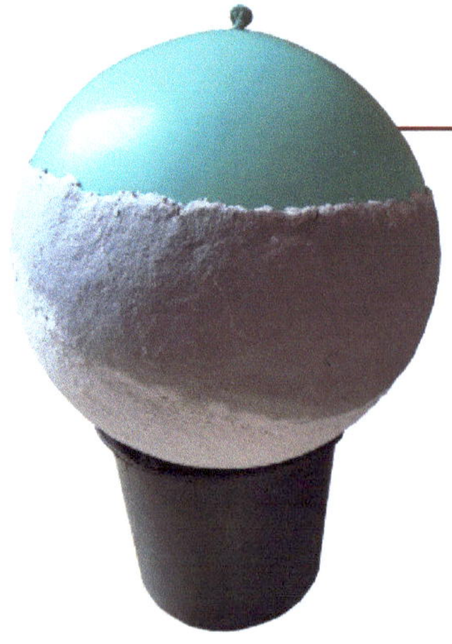

Spread the Papier-mâché layer up to about half of the balloon and only to the maximum width before the balloon deflates again. The cup should have a typical tea cup shape and not become narrower at the top. After the first thin layer has dried, apply a second layer on top of the first so that you have a thickness of about 1 inch all over.

When the two layers are dried thoroughly, you can pop the balloon. Let it burst by using a needle. It then detaches itself from the edge and shrinks. We don't need it anymore.

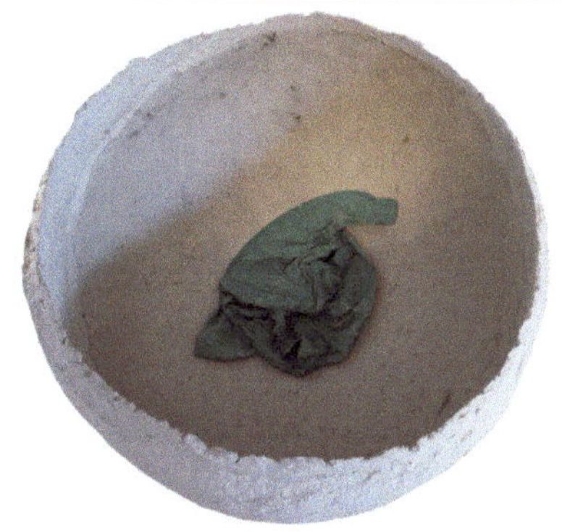

Now, smooth out any uneven areas by adding an additional layer of papier-mâché. Focus on leveling the surface, ensuring that the top edge is flat and even. This will give your project a more polished and professional finish. To check whether the edge is level, you can use a spirit level for precision or simply assess it by eye if you don't have one on hand. Taking the time to perfect this step will ensure the final result looks neat and well-balanced.

Perhaps you want to form the rim of the cup like a classic teacup, then you arch it a bit more outwards.

Apply more papier-mâché until the cup has a thickness of approximately 1 inch and let it dry for about ten days.

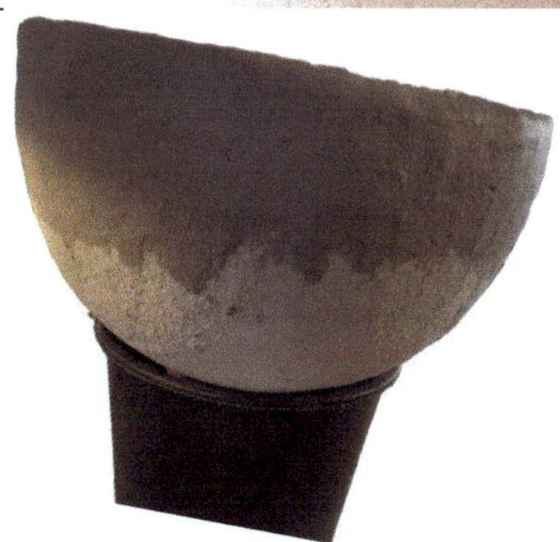

Now we are going to attach a base under the corpus. For this I cut off the edge of a small bucket and attach it with hot glue and tape. But you can also cut a border out of thicker cardboard. Then the inside and outside of the edge is covered with papier-mâché. It is important that you attach it neatly in the middle and that everything is straight.

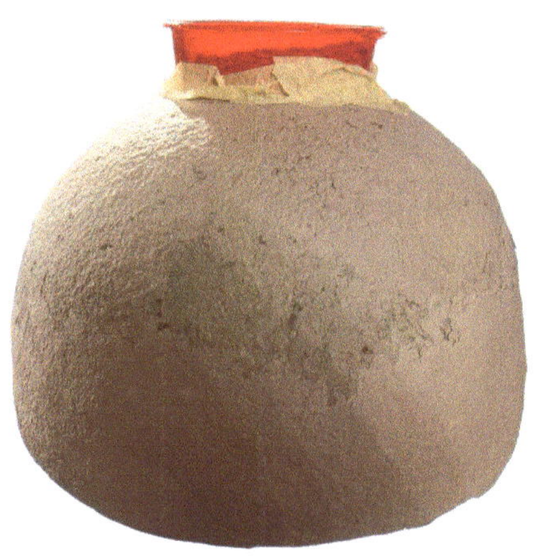

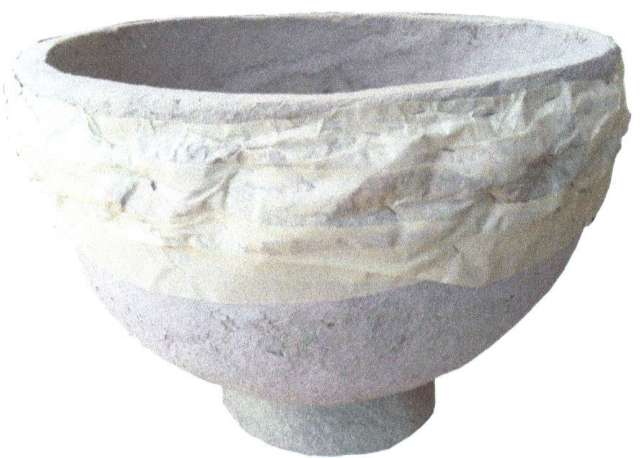

You can add several layers of papier-mâché – until you are satisfied with the result.
If a slightly thicker layer is to be applied, you can also attach crumpled newspaper with a stapler and attach it with adhesive tape. This saves papier-mâché and drying time.

Now form a handle out of robust wire. The best thing to do is to double the wire and use round-nose pliers to form eyelets at both ends, which we will use later to attach the screws.

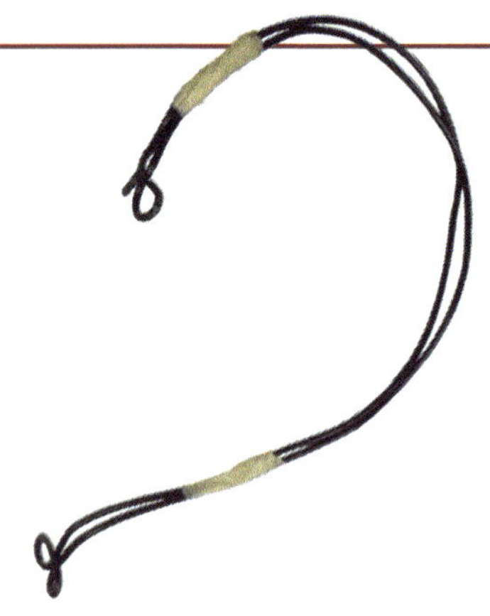

Attach the handle tot he cup.
Wrap some adhesive tape
around it and then apply a first
layer of papiermache to he
handle and the points where it
meets the body of the teacup.

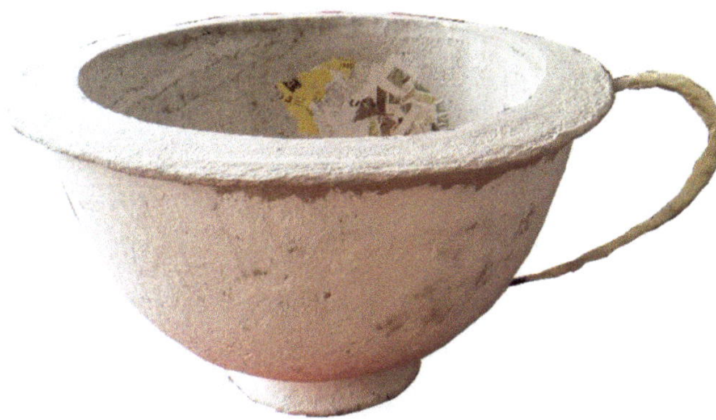

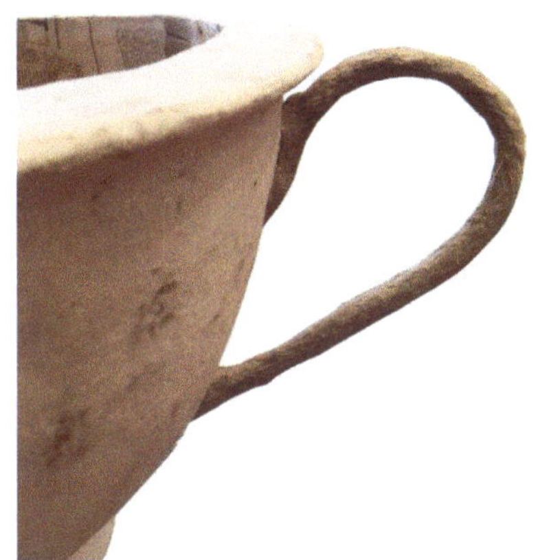

The first moist papiermache layer
might well slide away when applied
the the handle. Therefore I would
recommend to take this process in
steps. Once the first layer has dried
you can proceed to form the handle to
your liking.

Fort he table area I took a cardboard template, which I transferred to

plywood and cut it out. In ordert to have a rim

around my table area I positioned the lid a

little deeper. For this purpose you need to

attach a holding structure to the inside of

the cup on which the lid will rest. You can fix

the wooden lid tightly to he corpus or you just

leave it like it is so that you can open and close it.

The other option which is also easier: Cut a wooden lid which is placed on top oft he cup and fix it with masking tape

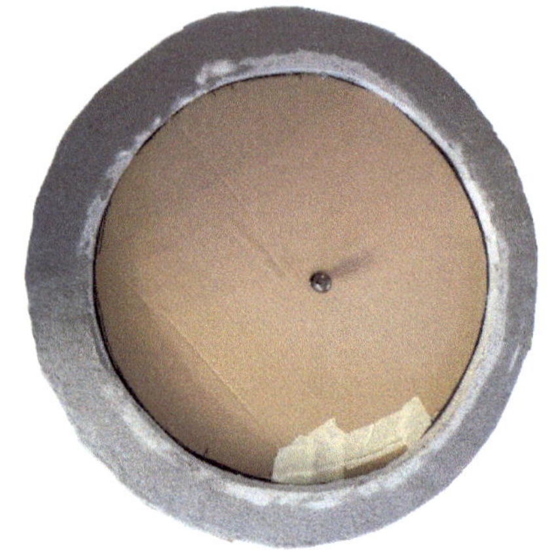

To make it easy to lift and lower the lid, you can attach a doorknob or a similar object to serve as a handle. However, for a more creative and playful touch, consider modeling a small figure or object around the knob. For instance, you could craft a tiny sugar pot, a whimsical animal, or any shape that suits the design of your teapot. This not only makes the lid functional but also adds a unique and personal decorative element to your piece, turning it into a charming work of art.

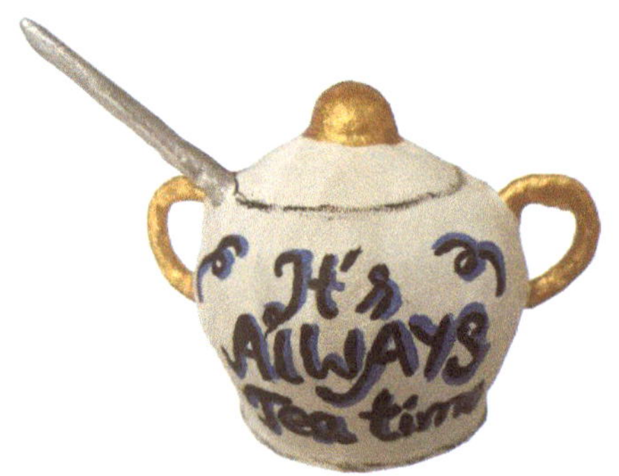

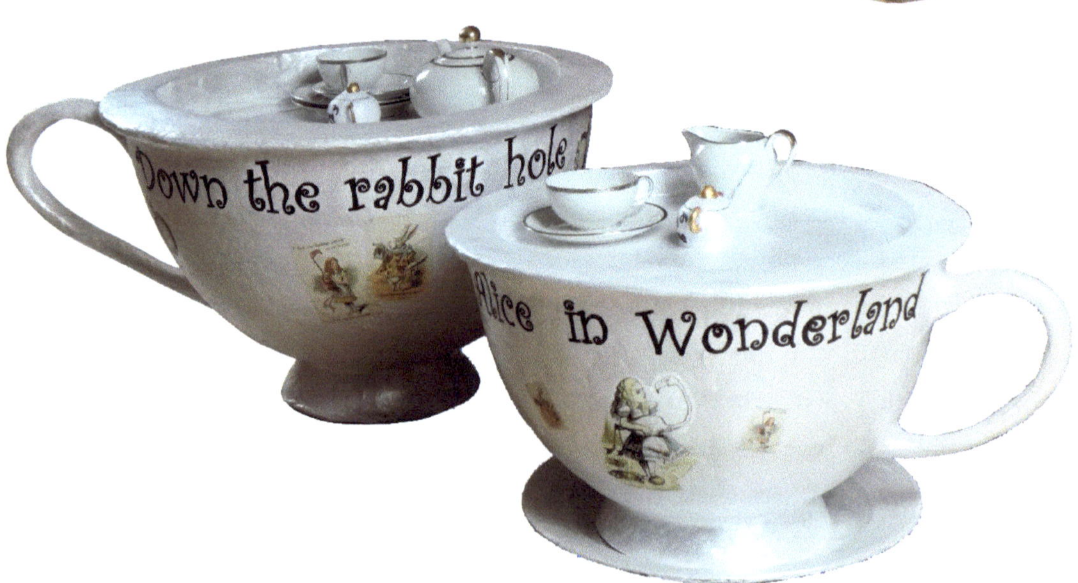

More ideas for designs with balloons used as substructure:

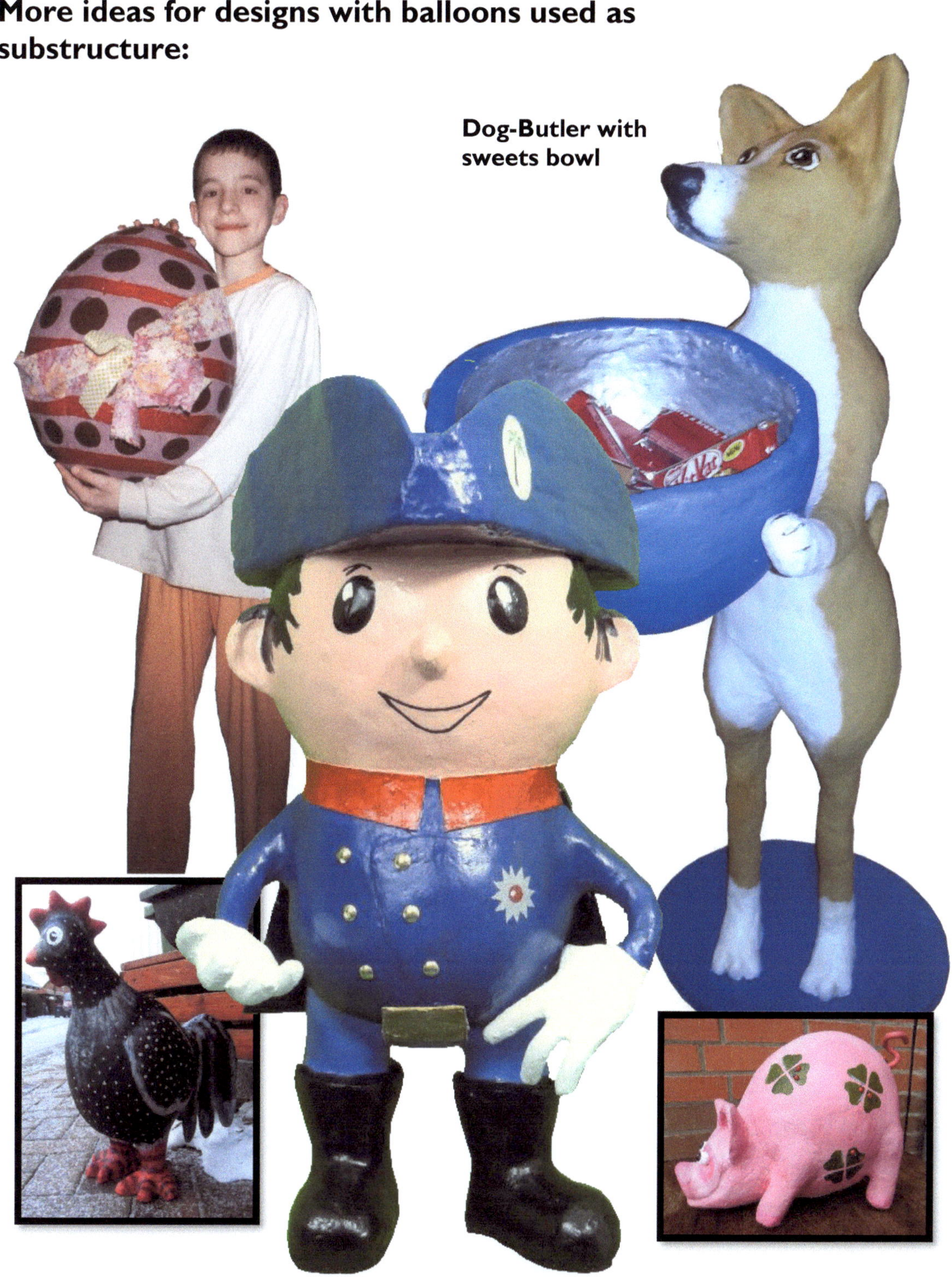

CHAPTER 4

Medium sized sculptures

with wire skeleton

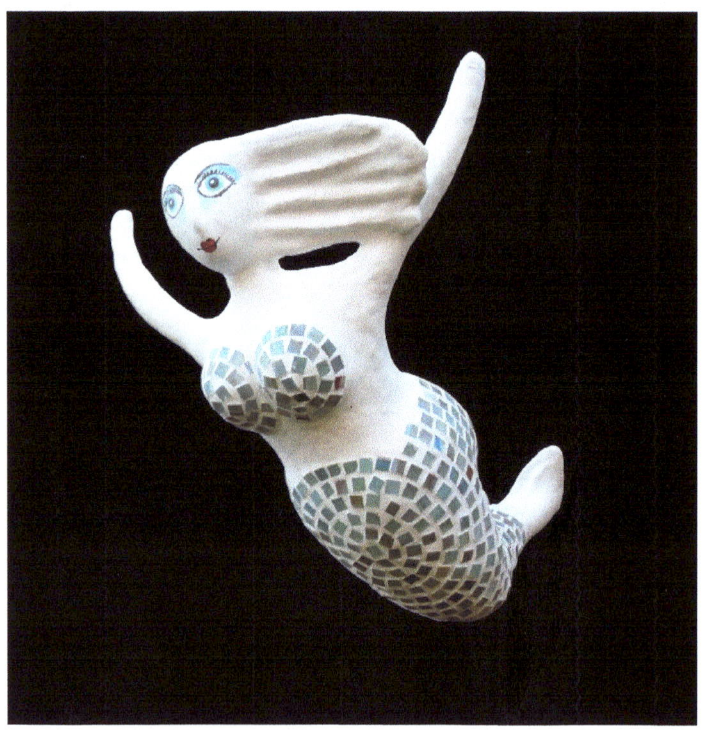

Medium sized sculptures

Do you wish to create something standing or sitting upright or in any other special composure? In order to achieve that scrunch newspaper and wrap chicken wire around it. This will give stability and makes it possible to form details.

Of course it is also possible to take all other household items as substructure which you've always wanted to get rid of, such as an awful vase (last Christmas present from Aunt Mable) you want to turn into a modern and rather stylish vase. Or you might want to put an empty gherkin glas in the centre of your new substructure. If you need some weight to keep your piece of work stable and prevent it to top over by the wind just put stones or gravel into the empty gherkin glas.

Transform the cardboard box of your blueray player into a crazy shelf or turn an empty bottle of wine into a plump mermaid.

You can either use the item as a skeleton, that means it will stay inside your figure. But if you want to keep the item use the given design and form an imprint like copying a big bowl for plants out of the imprint of a gymnastic ball! But be sure to cover the item with some kind of release agent like Vaseline before covering it with pulp. It will be easier to disconnect the dried form from it.

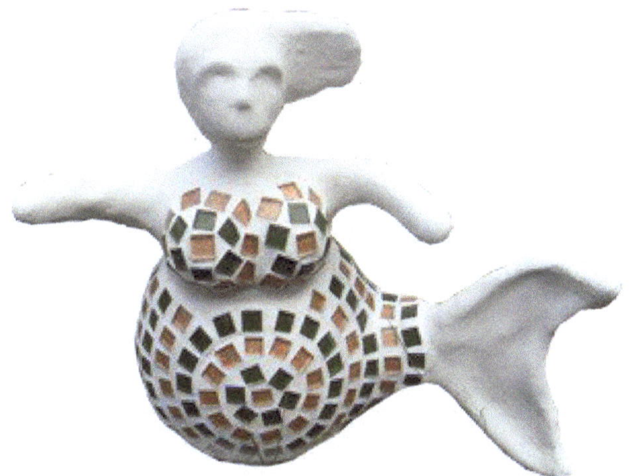

This is what you will need for a "Mermaid"

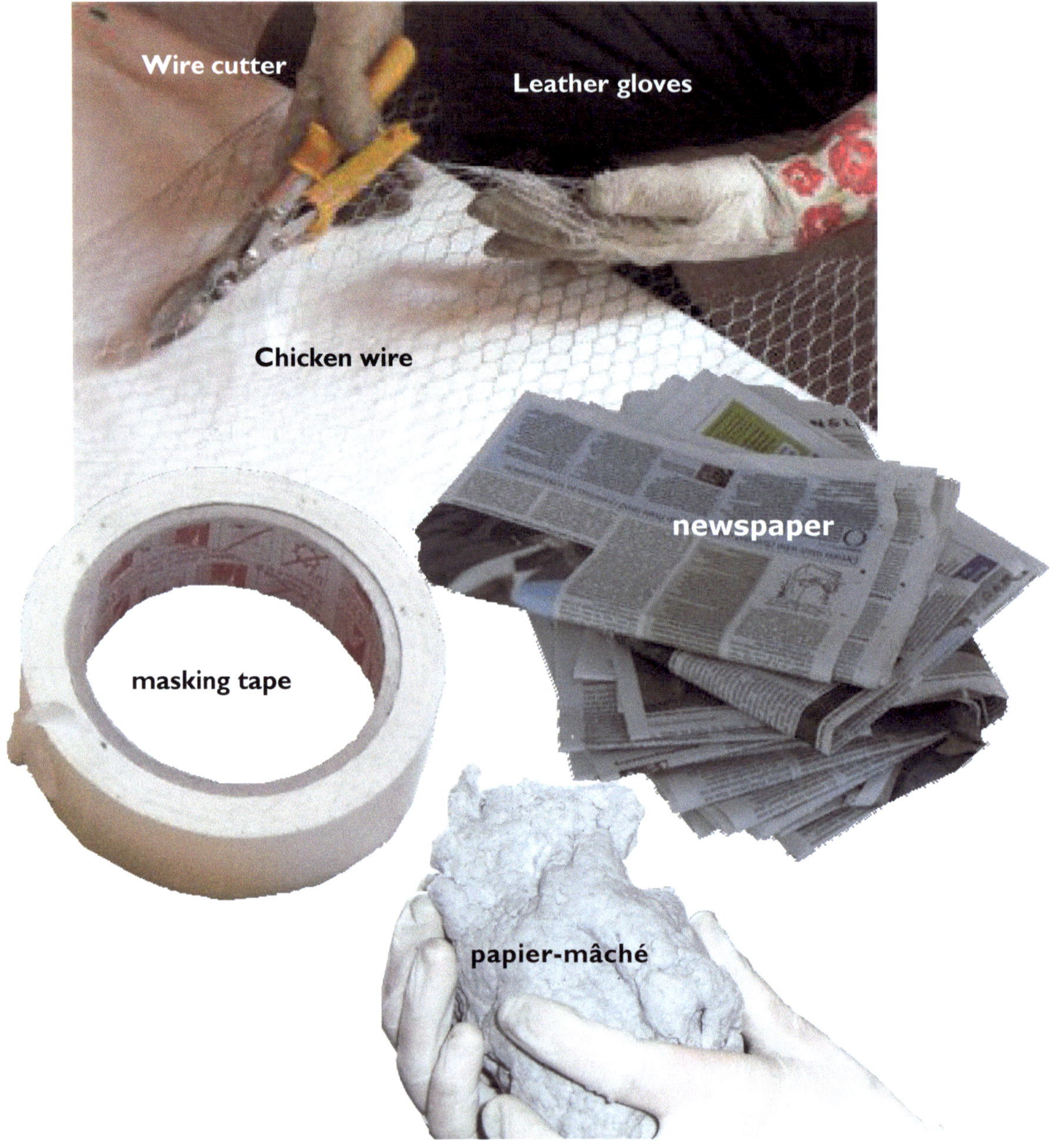

Step-by-Step

The Mermaid

Here, we need a simple frame made of wire mesh, which can be easily purchased at any hardware store. There are various qualities of chicken wire available, but I recommend using hexagonal wire mesh as it is particularly easy to shape by hand. Be sure to choose a medium mesh size: if the gaps are too large, precise shaping can become tricky, while gaps that are too small might make bending and twisting the wire unnecessarily difficult. Using a wire cutter, carefully cut a rectangular piece measuring 15 x 20 inches for the best results.

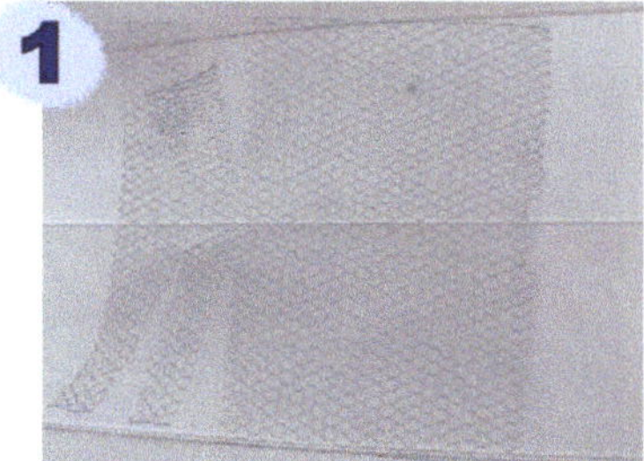

Cut it as shown here. Please make sure to wear leather protective gloves as chicken wire has sharp ends and may easily hurt you.

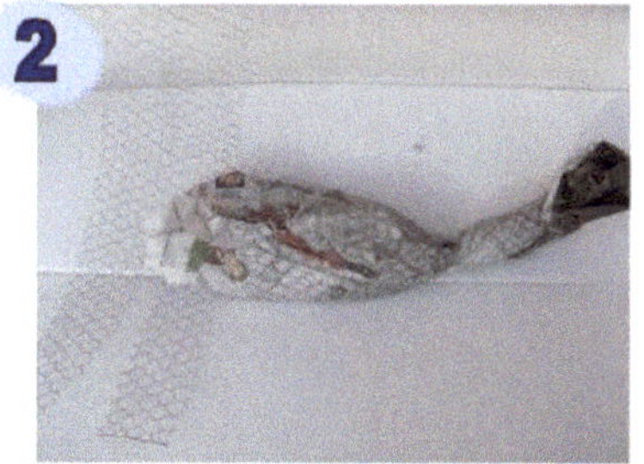

Put some compressed newspaper "sausages" into the middle of the form and fold the lower pieces of meshwork into the middle. Press the meshwork firmly into a roundish form.

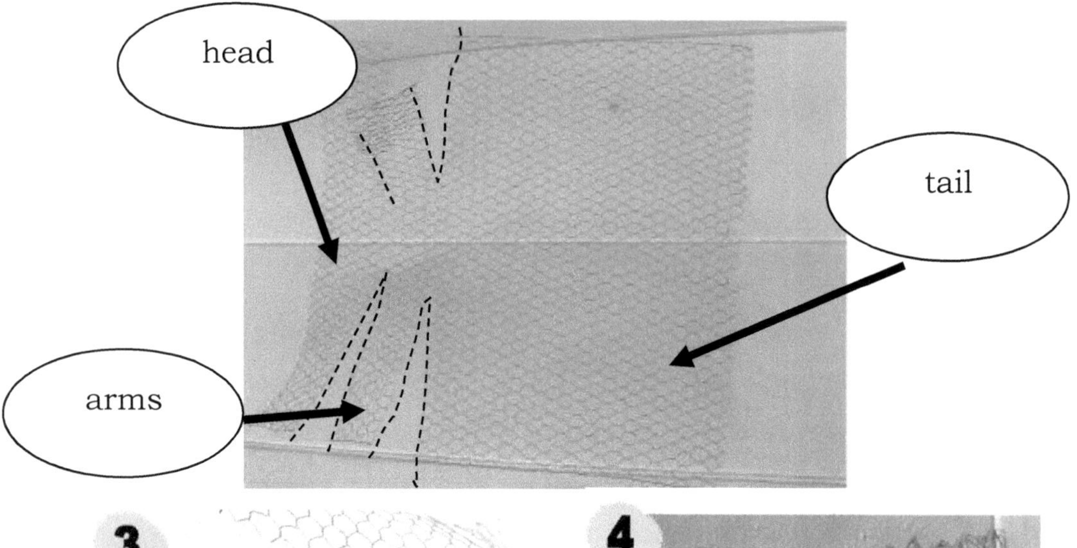

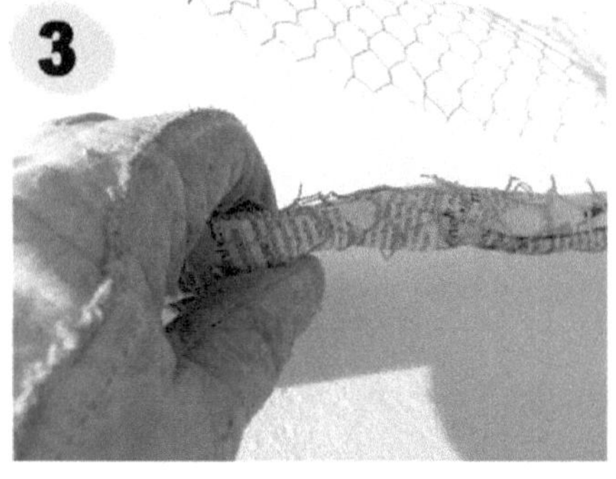

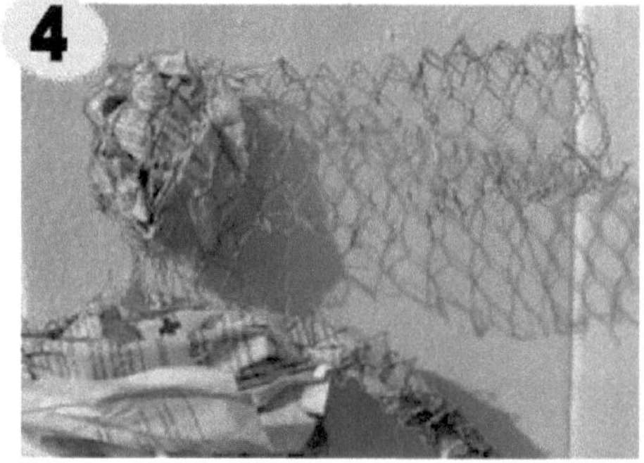

Press newspaper into a tight role which you then push into the armpipes. If you put a relatively hard wire at the centre of tightly fixed newspaper snippets and wrap them with chicken wire you will later be able to bend and rotate the arm in the desired position before you apply papier-mâché. Fin-like hands fit perfectly to this mermaid, so don't bother forming fingers or fists. Just let the arms go thinner where you would expect the hands.

Now fold around one side of the hair so that it comes to lie on the other half. Bend the edges according to your personal taste. There is no standard, follow your own ideas. Stuff the head with newspaper

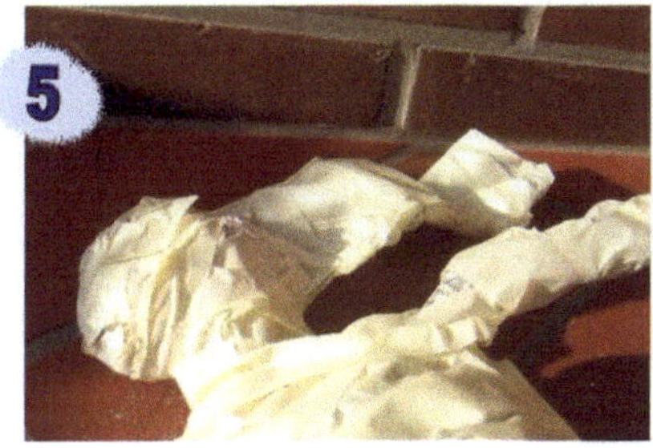

Now wrap the whole figure with tape. That keeps the chicken wire together and avoids the pulp from falling through the gaps into the chicken wire.

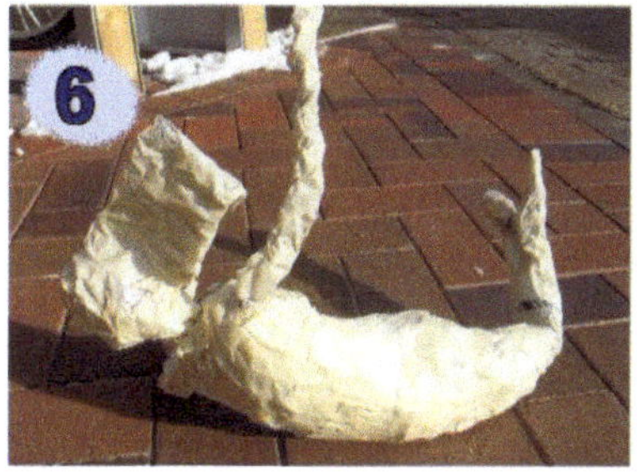

If you want, you can also change the appearance of the mermaid, for example try to bend the arms back. Due to the chicken wire they will remain in that position.

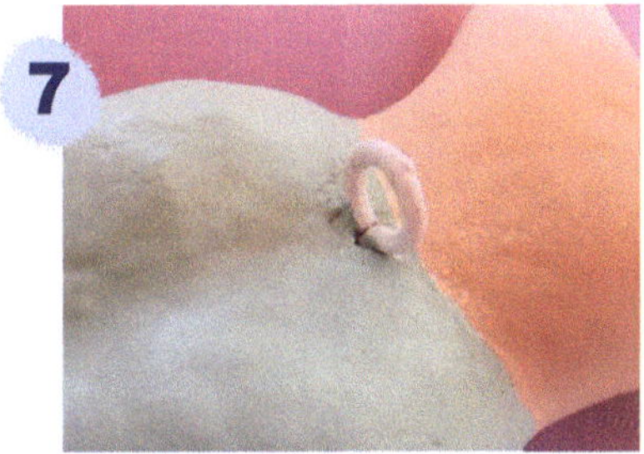

Don't forget to include a sturdy hook. If you plan to add mosaic stones to the final design, ensure the hook can support the added weight. Ideally, integrate the loop into the substructure before applying papier-mâché, leaving part of it exposed through all layers. If you forget, attach the hook securely after drying, embedding it deep into the papier-mâché. Position the hook carefully to ensure she hangs balanced from the ceiling.

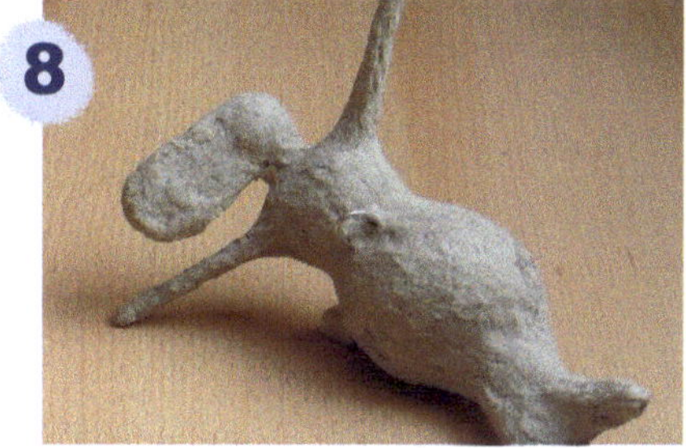

Now cover the base/structure with papier-mâché, possibly in several steps, giving time to let each layer dry off thoroughly. Since the first layer will inevitably look rather bumpy it makes sense to let a second or even third layer follow to make a smooth surface. If you decide to cover the sculpture (partly) with mosaic stones additional layers are not necessary.

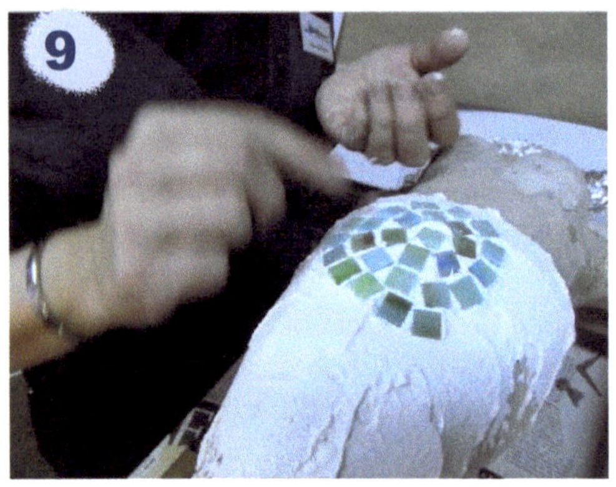

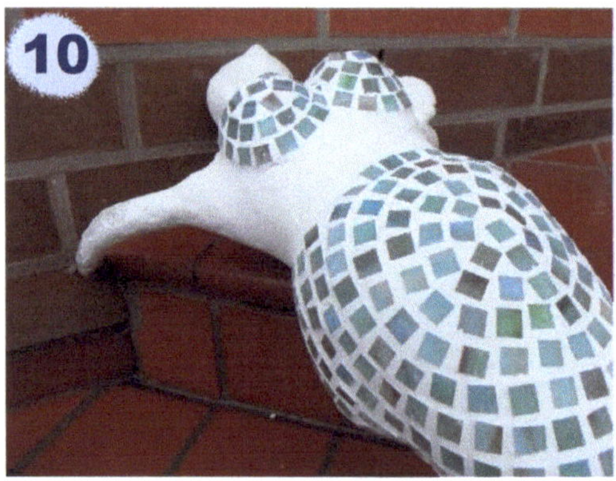

For this mermaid, I later added a vibrant mosaic, but you could also choose to paint it with acrylic colours if you prefer a simpler approach. Both options can result in a stunning final piece. If you decide to go with the mosaic,

everything you need can easily be found in a good DIY shop. In addition to the mosaic glass pieces, you'll need special adhesive and grout to secure and seal the surface effectively. Take care to attach a

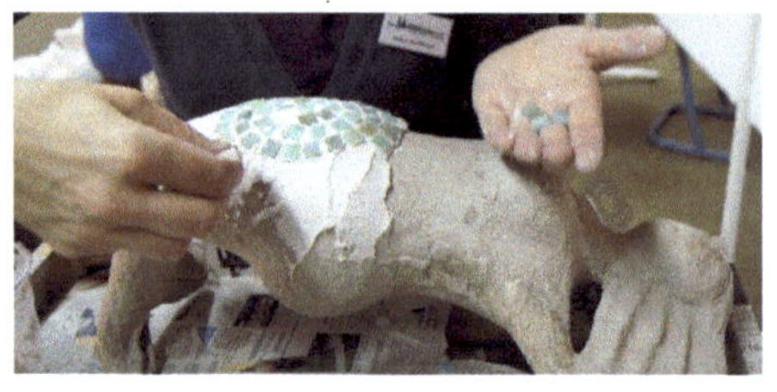

strong and reliable suspension, as the mosaic will add considerable weight to the figure, making sturdy support essential.

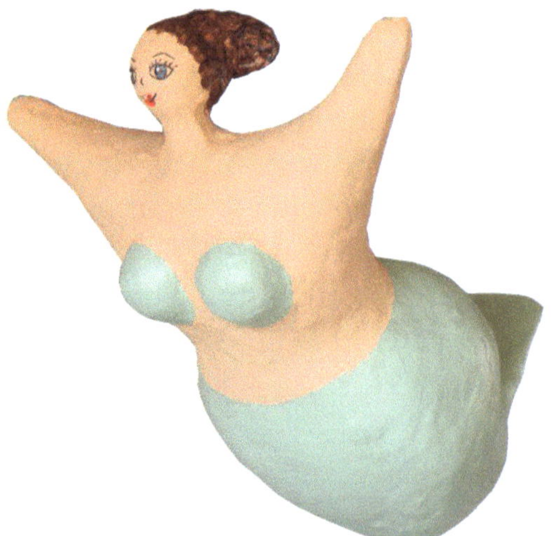

When applying mosaic it is important to make sure that the figure underneath has completely dried off. If moisture remains in the material cracks will occur in the glue during the drying process.

More examples for figures that require a wire frame

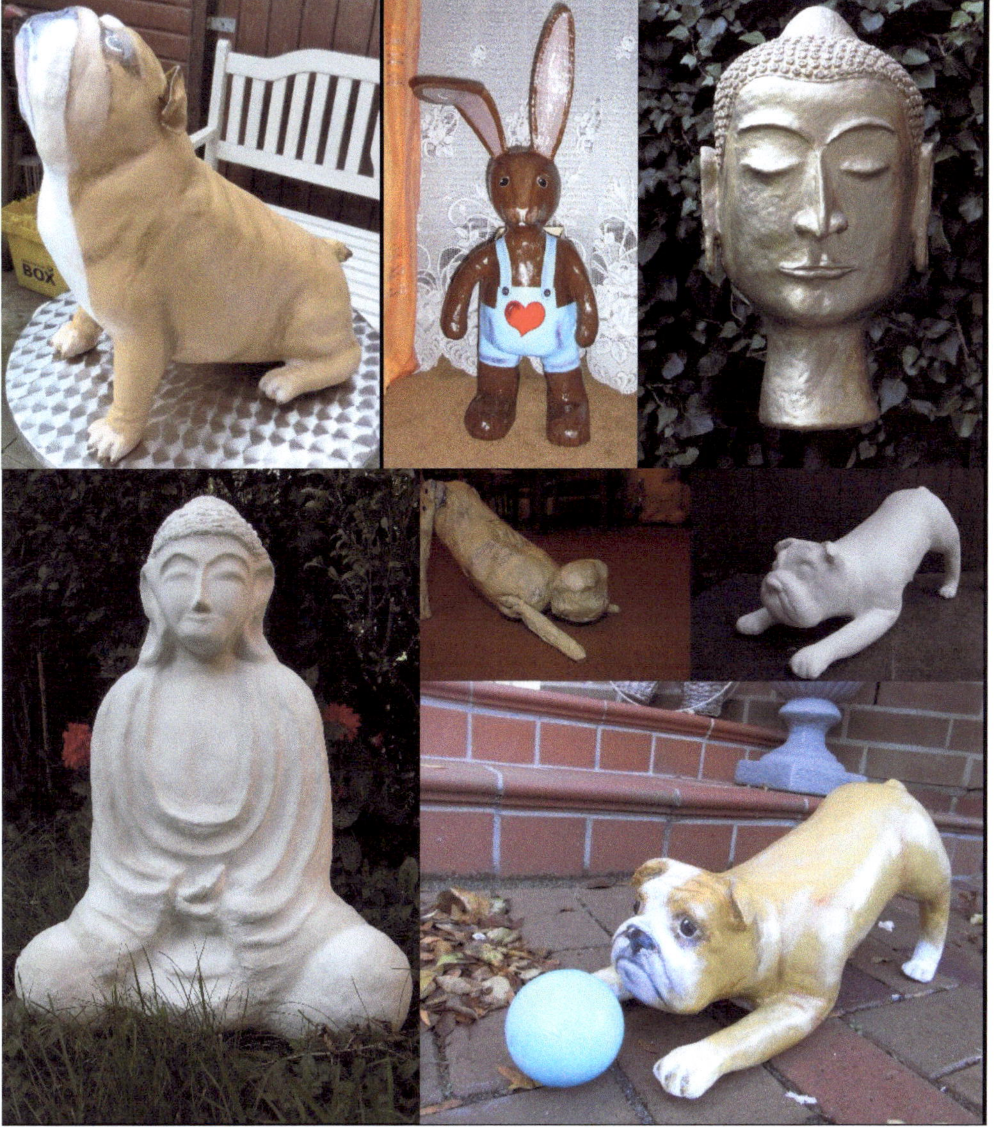

CHAPTER 5

Large Figures on

a wooden frame:

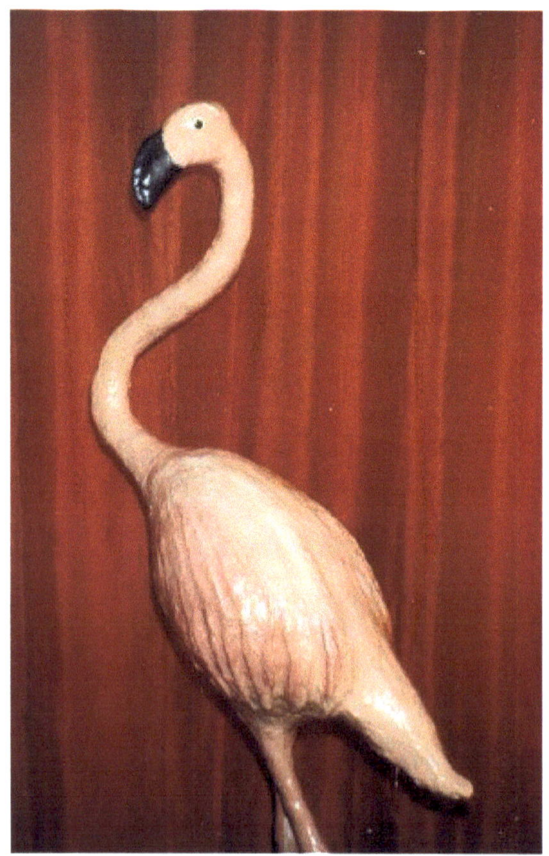

Larger figures

For larger sculptures, it's essential to create an exceptionally stable framework. This stability is critical because the drying process can take quite some time, and any sagging must be avoided during this period. Papier-mâché is heavy when wet, exerting significant pressure on the structure. The larger the sculpture and the more papier-mâché you apply, the more vital it becomes to construct a robust and secure base. This is why a wooden framework is highly recommended. Rabbit wire can be easily attached to the wooden frame, providing a foundation for adding buffer materials such as paper, cardboard, or

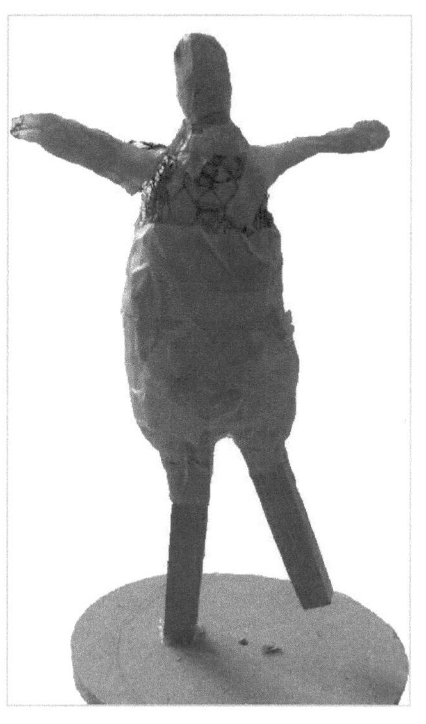

other fillers. However, it's important to avoid applying too much papier-mâché in one go. A layer approximately 1 inch thick is sufficient to achieve a wood-like texture. Anything thicker could result in the papier-mâché sagging or peeling away from the framework due to its weight.

Start by cutting a wooden board into any shape you desire as the base. Attach two rails to this board, adjusting their placement to match the form of the figure you're building. For smaller or simpler sculptures, it may suffice to screw two vertical beams onto the wooden base. For larger and more complex figures, however, it's crucial to construct the entire posture of the sculpture at this early stage, ensuring a strong and stable structure as a foundation for your creative work.

How to plan your work of art

Look at the sculpture below: I cut 2 identical wooden rails which needed to be slightly longer than the intended height of the figure (since they were mounted diagonally). I screwed them onto the base so that they met at the top end and remained rather far apart at the bottom end. The lower part will later be legs and feet. Try to see your figure in this construction. Sometimes it might make sense to cross the rails where the neck of the figure is expected, so that the construction by the two rails is narrow for the neck and a bit wider for the head. The head will be fixed separately. Use your imagination. It is sufficient to screw the rails together with screws using a screwdriver.

The legs can be fixed on the board by metal angles. It does not matter how it looks, because in a second step the framework is covered with papier-mâché. The most important thing is the stability of the framework. I prefer to work with wood, as it is easy to work with. Sometimes I keep old screws from shelves etc. to recycle them for later art work.You can use solid wire just as well, which you can find in coat-hangers. With this kind of wire the figure is very stable and does not bend if you cover it with papier-mâché.

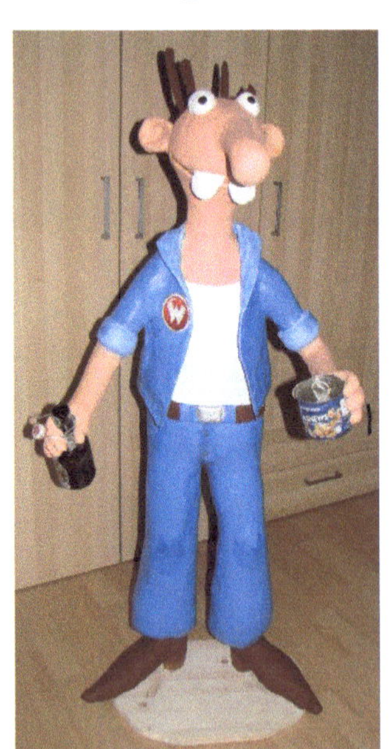

Why not create your children's favourite hero using papier-mâché? Just imagine their delight when their beloved comic book character appears as a lamp, a playful decoration, or even a whimsical butler, ready to greet them at the birthday table! Alternatively, you could craft a life-sized replica of your dog, bringing your furry friend to life in a unique and artistic way.

To start, use a photo or printout as a reference for the shape and details of your creation an plan the appropriate substructure carefully. Keep in mind that smaller figures require less support from their substructure, making them easier to construct. With a bit of creativity and preparation, you'll be able to craft a wonderful piece that will amaze and delight! Depending on the form, posture and kind of

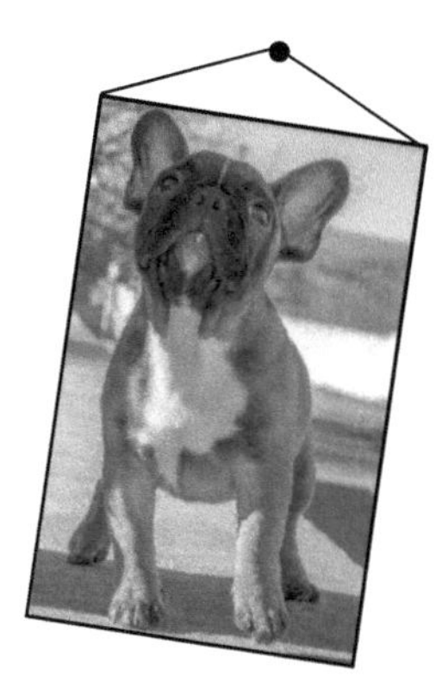

sculpture we need to choose an adequately formed substructure which fits to the form of our piece of art, i.e. the wooden framework should stabilize and support the figure in its posture. Please see the following drawings for illustration.

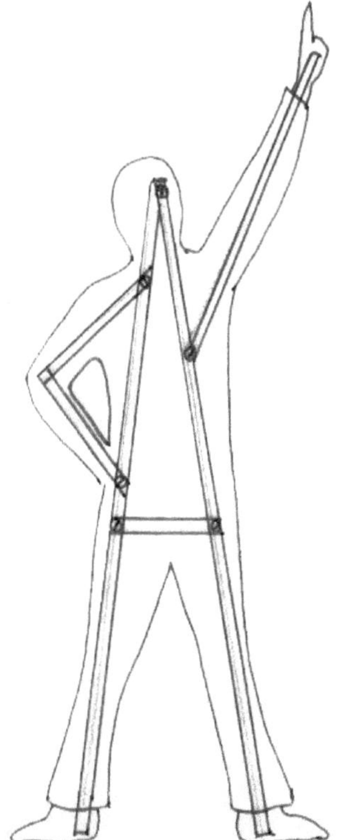

The underlying structure for a human sculpture was formed by joining two beams and fixing them to each other on the top. In the middle we mounted a cross-bar to gain stability. The arm reaching up as well as the bent arm are fixed to the latches. At this point it is not relevant how the armature looks since everything will be covered with papier-mâché later. Fix the latches with two screws (one is not enough since the latch will start turning when the weight of the papier-mâché is added)

These proceedings are quite similar with the elephant (representative for any other figure with a similar posture) and the Flamingo. At the end of both the neck of the flamingo and the trunk of the elephant I attached strong wire to the latch to form the curve. This is easier than to work with wood for this purpose. Next you scrunch paper, wrap it around the wire and fix it with sticky tape.

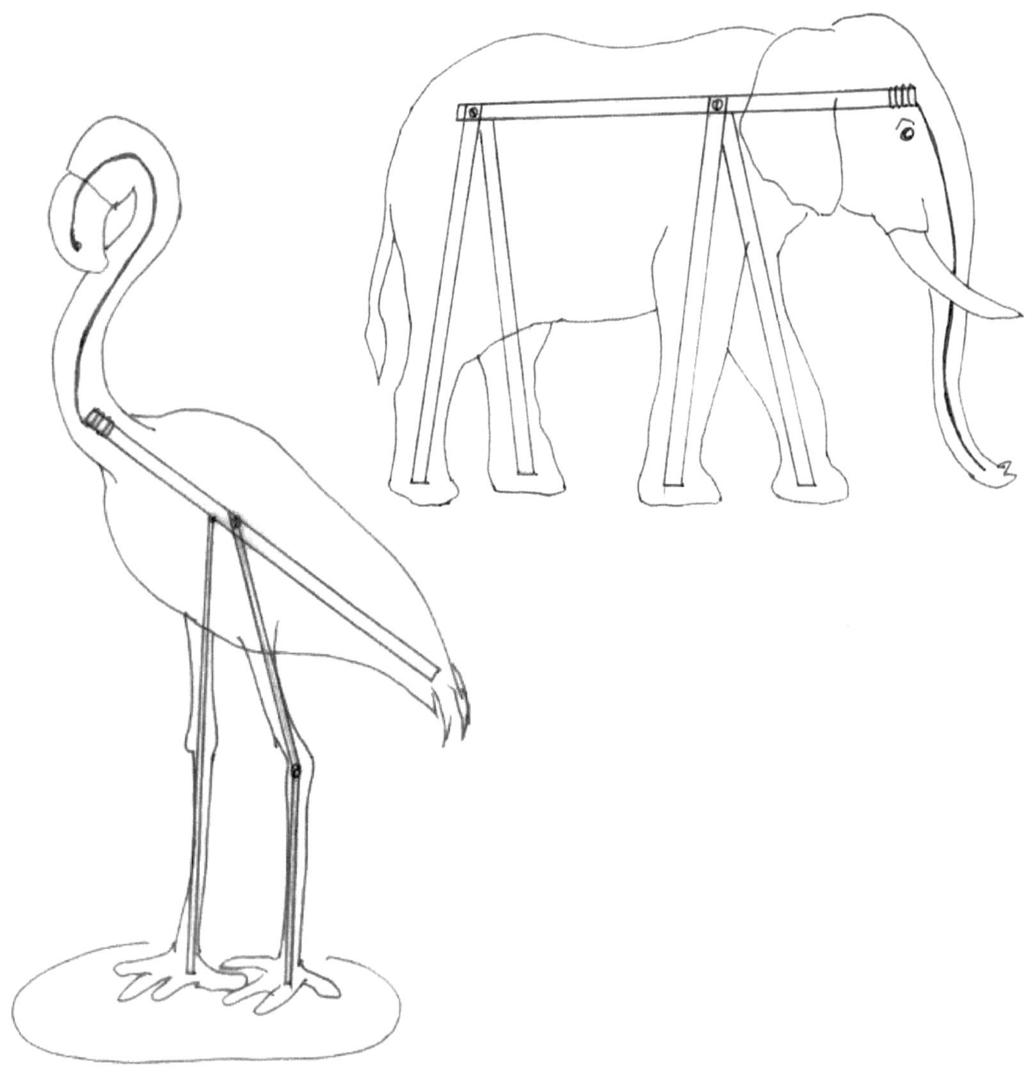

How to model a figure based on a photo

As seen before large lifesize sculptures have to be robust and need a lot of stability. Every element that extends outward from your figure requires a sturdy supporting framework. At first, this might feel a bit challenging, as you need to think ahead about how the finished piece will look. However, you'll quickly adapt and start spotting potential materials from your surroundings.-.whether household items or everyday objects.-.that can serve as excellent structural supports. For example, ears and wings can be cut from sturdy cardboard and securely attached to the form. Wire coat hangers or wooden skewers for kebabs can be used to stabilise certain parts. Once I even sacrificed a kitchen fork to hold an arm in place, as it was under considerable tension!

When I first started working with papier-mâché, I often felt frustrated by the need to plan and stabilise everything beforehand. My impatience made me want to dive straight into building the figure. Over time, I learned that the durability and quality of papier-mâché sculptures heavily depend on a well-constructed framework. Now, I take great care and pour a lot of thought and love into this foundational step. Not only does a robust framework enhance the longevity of your piece, but it also reduces the amount of papier-mâché you need to use.

To begin, print a picture of the figure you wish to create and sketch the substructure directly onto it. As shown in the examples on the previous page, this will give you a clear plan. Once the structure is drawn, decide on the size you want your sculpture to be. Moving from a two-dimensional drawing to a three-dimensional figure might sound daunting at first, but with a bit of imagination and creativity, you'll find it easier than you expect to envision and craft the unseen parts, bringing your design to life!

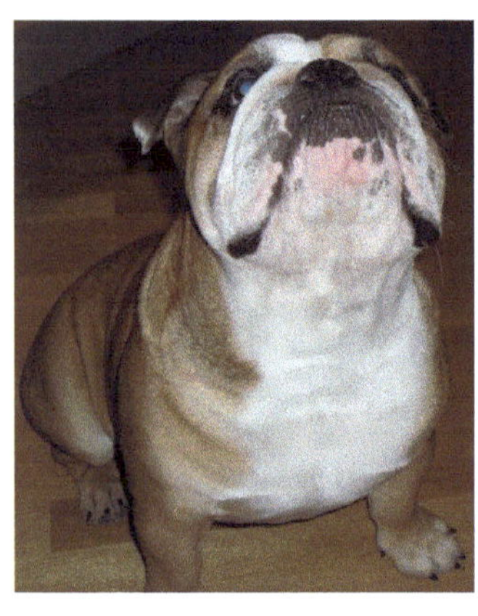

Now plan the proportions. To give you an example: I formed a dog of about 60 cm in height from a photograph. In order to transfer the proportions shown on the photo we will have to do a little calculation. Take a ruler and measure the distance from head to toe (in this case 15 cm) Divide the intended size (here 60 cm) by the size of it on the print (in this case 60 cm / 15 cm = 4 cm). You get the scale 1 : 4 i.e. 4 cm on the sculpture counts for 1 cm on the printed image

By applying a grid pattern to the picture you are able to transfer the proportions to your substructure. I always put a "ruler" of the final size at the centre of my planned figure and apply every part of the body. Each mark represents a paw, thigh, chest, shoulder, head etc. Always applying the scale 1:4

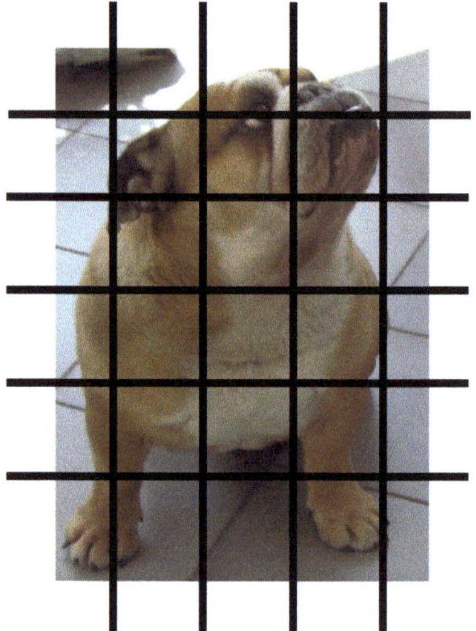

Nose

Neck

Tail

Paws

With my „ruler"a wooden latch I mark some parts of the body in proportion. Using the grid it is easy to transfer sizes onto our sculpture in scale

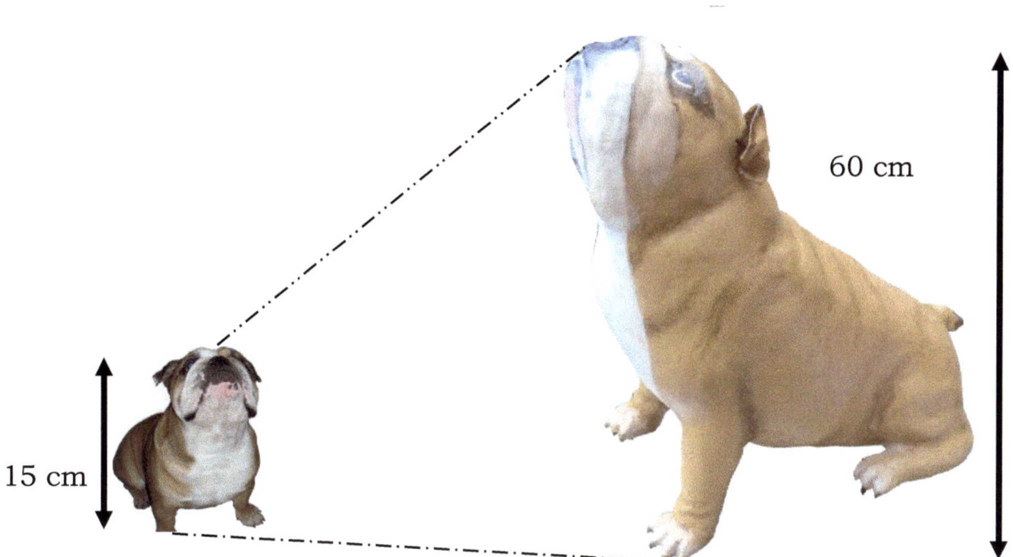

When creating an upright standing sculpture it helps to fix it to a base plate to keep it from falling over. It is easier that way rather than balancing it on its feet. Especially when applying the wet papier-mâché or modelling it, the base plate stabilizes the figure.

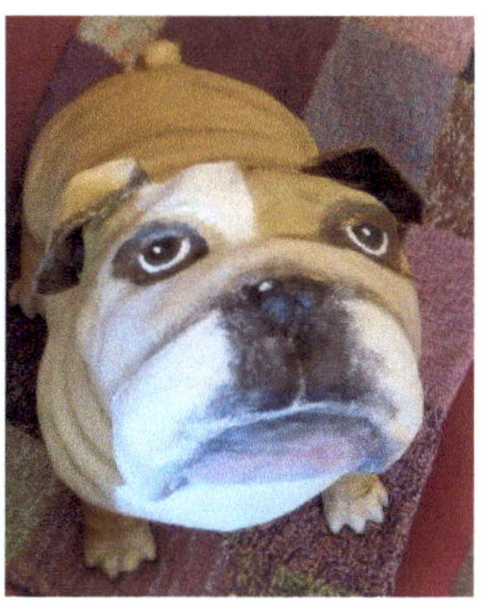

For this dog, you won't need a base plate, as it sits naturally on its hind legs. I shaped the front legs around DIY latches, which I assembled and screwed together (see the chapter on "Substructure"). I continued this process for the entire substructure, carefully adhering to the 1:4 scale throughout. What do you think? Are you ready to try a simple latch as a makeshift "ruler" to help mark the proportions?

Depending on your intentions you can also create a functional sculpture for example a figure holding a (dinner) tray – as a butler would do. Or a figure which can be used as coatrack or a lamp. There are no limits to your fantasy.

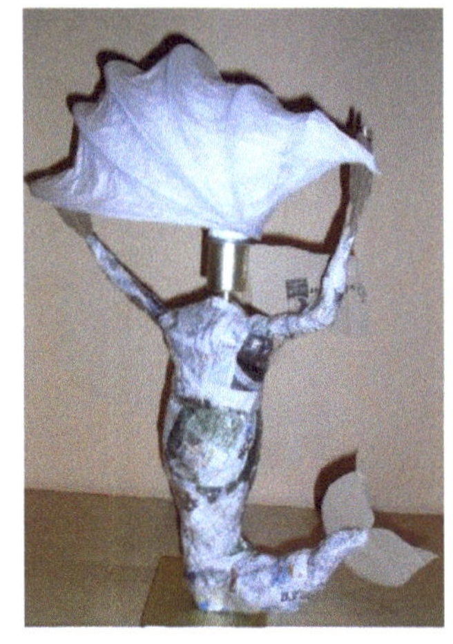

When you have finished your substructure use newspaper strips wrapping it around the frame forming the base figure as detailed as possible. The more detailed you work at this point the less papier-mâché you will need later and the faster your figure will dry. Preparing the substructure carefully and well will pay off. Basically you can use everything to be found in a normal household: toilet roll, newspaper, cardboard. Everything is being wrapped and attached around the wooden structure and fixed with sticky tape until you have almost created the sculpture as you want it.

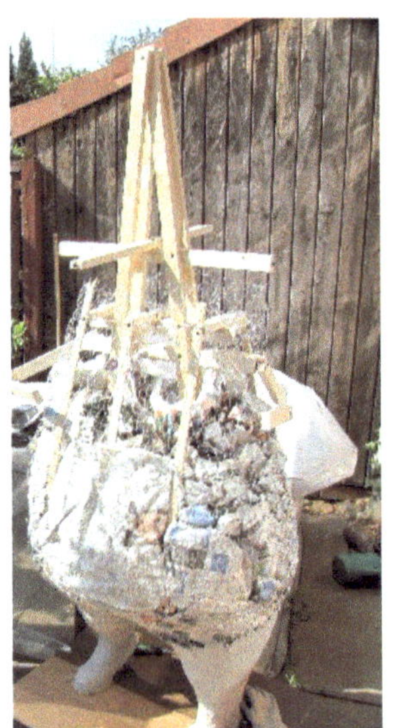

The belly of this 5,9 ft pig (see picture left) holds cardboard, empty corn Flakes boxes, newspaper etc. inside. Especially extremities like arms must be fixed to the frame firmly – even mor so if they have to support anything or you plan for them to carry something like a tray. Also ears, nose, things to be held have to be modelled from wire and paper wrapped around it so that the papier-mâché applied later does not slide off. Most important thin or delicate parts, eg. throats need a

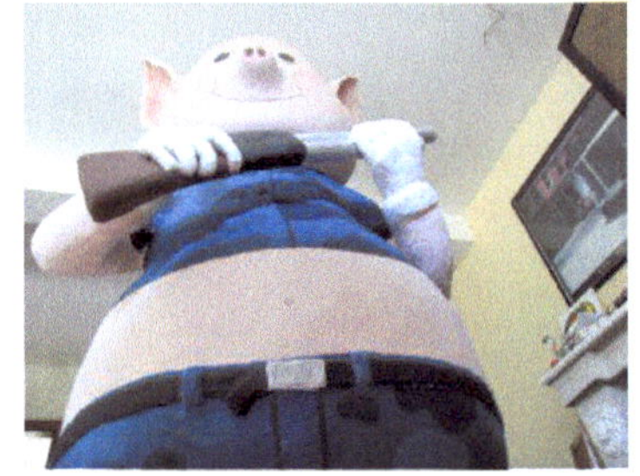

robust centre so they do not break.

This may not sound too exciting, I know. I do prefer starting to model immediately myself. But I assure you that a sound frame is most important to the whole structure.

Only when the basic structure is complete it makes sense to apply a layer of papier-mâché. And really: it is not important if the framework does not quite look like you expected it to be – it is only the first layer. All following layers will bring the figure nearer to your envisaged design. Is it still too slim? No problem, just add crunched newspaper to the dried form and fix it using sticky tape, screws etc. and give it a real good tummy.

Well, here you are, the frame is finished. Now start adding papier-mâché . For larger stretches of surface use a simple household knife to distribute the material across the structure. Make sure that the layers are not thicker than 1 inch because otherwise it might be difficult for it to dry. In that case you run the risk of mould occurring and the papier-mâché may then develop a foul smell.

In this picture you see the neck of a lifesize figure being repaired using screws. The substructure was not strong enough
to support the weight of the head.

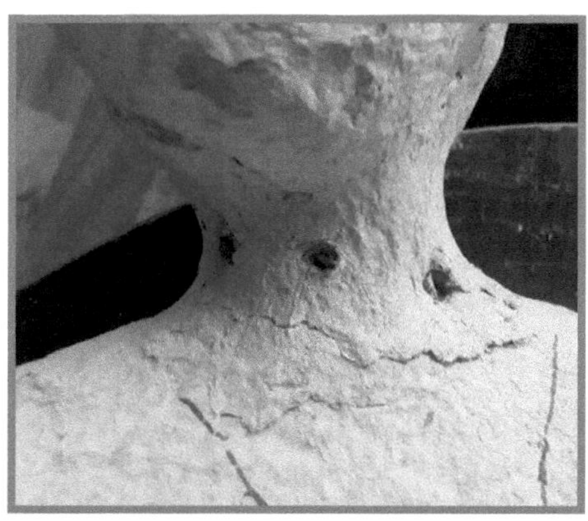

Jack, the sailor

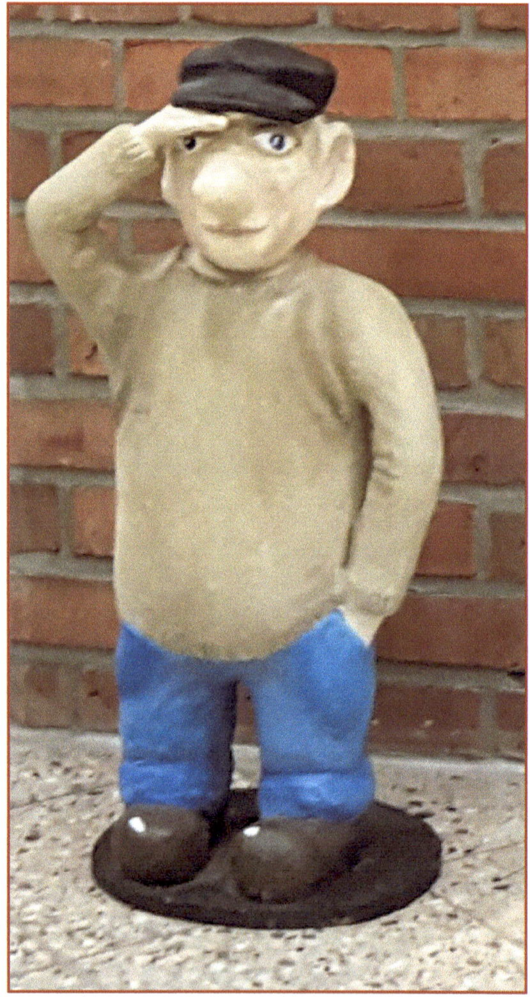

Step by step – the sailor

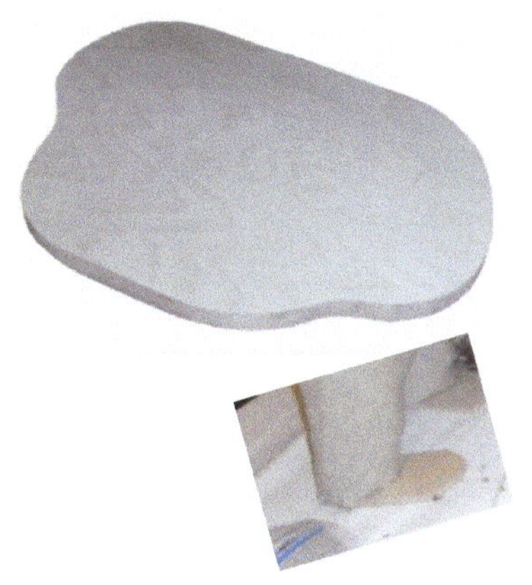

If the sailor needs a very safe stand I suggest to use glued laminated timber (glulam) of approx. 1,5 cm. It is quite reasonable since you can frequently find suitable pieces as waste or clipping in the wood department of your local building center and it does not swell easily when getting damp. If you want to have him stand on his own two feet saw two foot shaped support plates out of plywood and model to foot later with pulp..

Fix two ledgers to the support plate using angle pieces. Alternatively you could drill a long screw through the ledger directly into the floor plate.

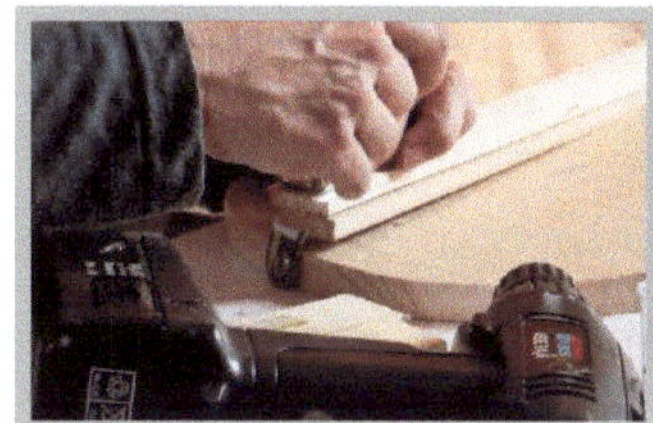
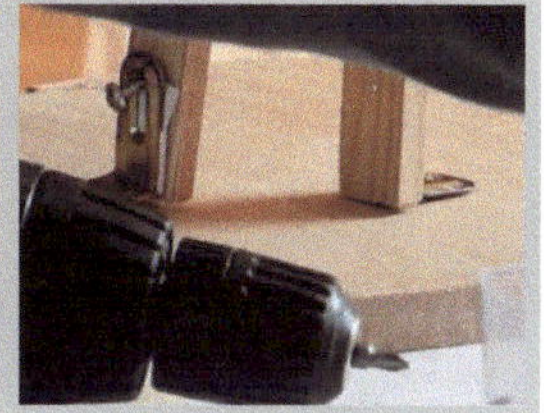

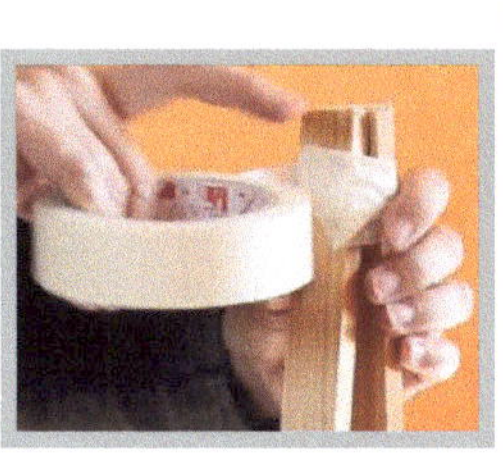
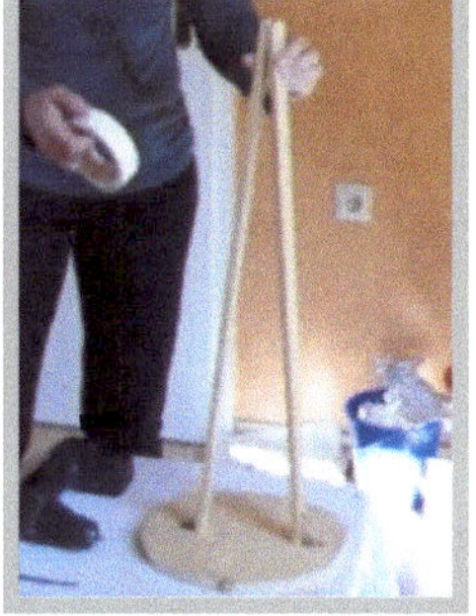

The two ledgers are held together using sticky tape. Tip: With a thick feltpen you can highlight the future positions of feet, knees, hip and shoulder on the wood.

For the shoulder you need a horizontal stick. Beware: the ledgers need preparational drill holes otherwise they split easily when the screws are pushed through unprepared.

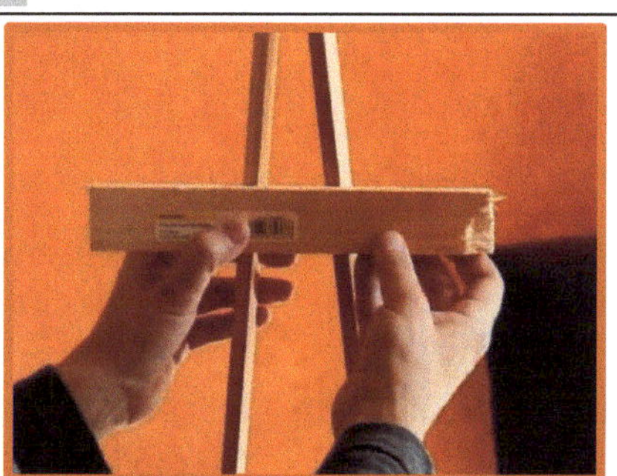

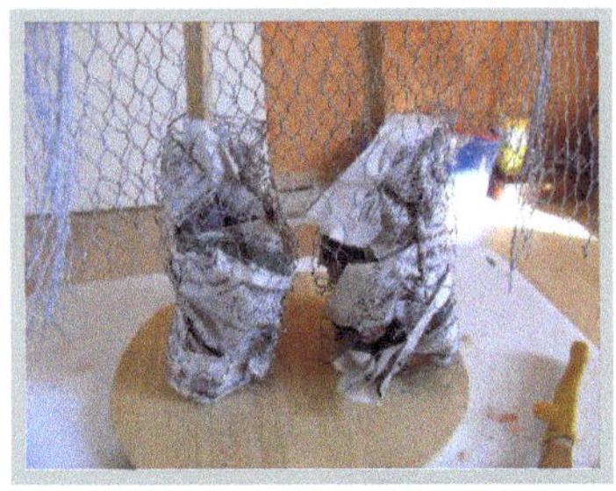

We wrap the lower end of the „legs" with newspaper and fasten it with stripes of wire mesh or very tight with sticky tape alternatively.

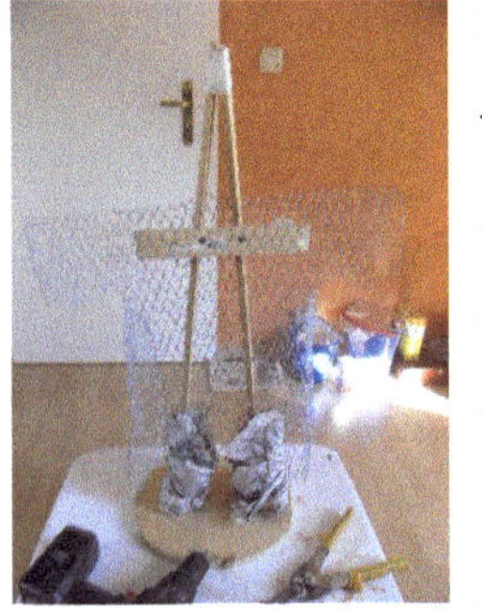

Start by cutting a rectangular piece of chicken wire, making a vertical slit in the centre so you can slip it over your figure like a pullover. Next, cut openings on both sides of the wire to create space for the figure's arms. At this stage, it should resemble a simple gown, and you'll already start to see the general shape of your figure taking form.

Once the wire is in place, stuff the structure generously with crumpled newspaper to give it volume. After stuffing, you can easily manipulate the chicken wire, pressing and shaping it to refine the figure's form. When you're satisfied with the shape, press the wire form firmly together and wrap it tightly with sticky tape to secure everything in place. For the arms, use what I call the "wringing technique." Hold the wire for one arm with both hands and twist the ends in opposite directions, just like wringing out a wet towel. This will compact the wire into a sturdy shape, ensuring the arm holds its position. Be careful to smooth out any bumps or sharp edges in the wire during this process, as uneven surfaces will be difficult to address later.

While papier-mâché can generally be sanded to a smooth finish after it has thoroughly dried, it becomes tricky if chicken wire or any other wire mesh is close to the surface. Taking extra care to prepare the structure now will save you time and effort later, ensuring a professional and polished end result

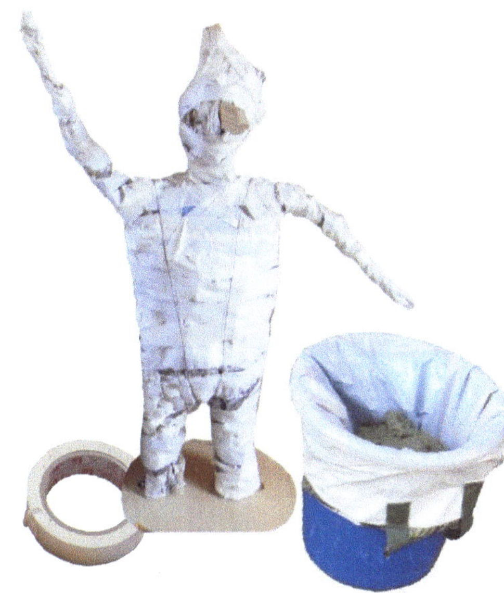

To form a big nose either use wire or fix a piece of wood in the appropriate place (see foto). You need this type of substructure in order to keep the pulp in place. Now the head: For my sailorman I decided to create a comic-like head. If you want to form a more realistic head and face, you will have to take into account other body dimensions. You would have to make sure that head and nose would be smaller and legs longer. In our example the sailor's head is exaggerated.

Subsequently the whole figure is wrapped in sticky tape firmly – just like a mummy. One of the arms you bend sharply where one would expect the elbow to be. The end of it – the hand – is fixed to the head by a screw. The other arm is bent down and fixed to the trousers. In the end it will disappear in the pocket. Now the time has come to spread pulp onto the sailor. It is best to do this in various steps so that each layer may dry thoroughly

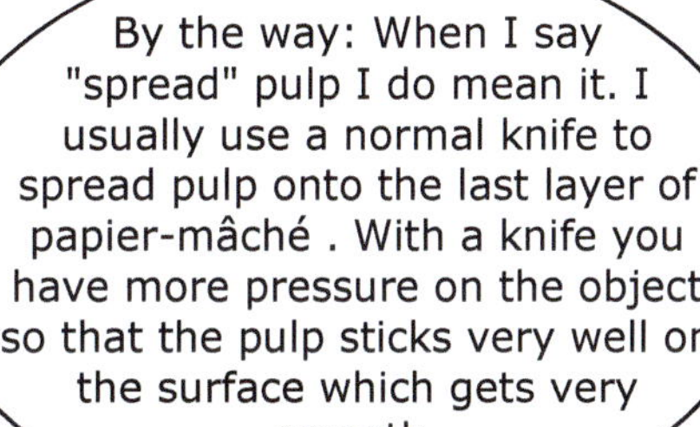

Now you are free to form the figure according to your ideas. You can also put a hat on the seaman's head.
The pullover of the sailor appears more vivid if you press a kind of knitting pattern onto the collar and the base as well as onto the wristband (when you work on the sleeves). By cutting into the sleeve with the back of a knife you can create "wrinkles" which looks very natural.

Later, when painting, you can use a slightly darker shade of colour to add to the effect

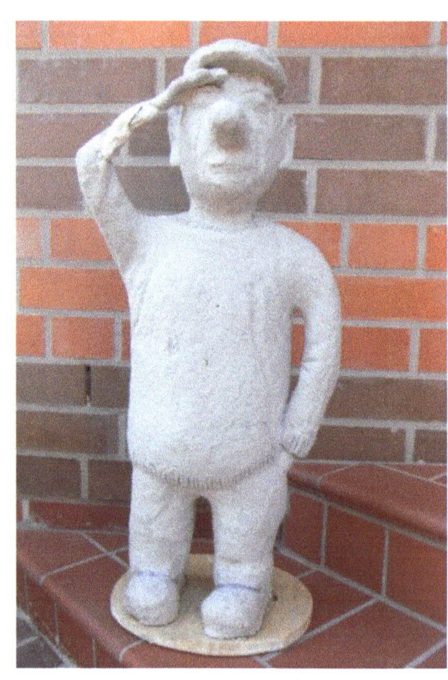

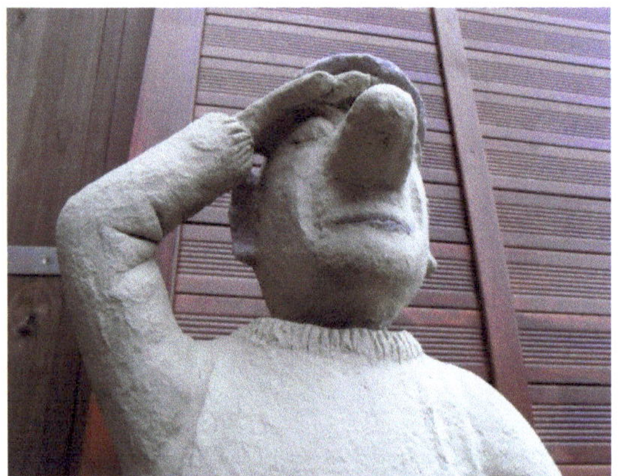

Once the head is dry bend the arm structure of the right arm so that the hand touches the forehead to give the impression that our sailor looks into the far distance. Perhaps you want to form the hand as if our sailor protects his eyes from the blazing sun. Fix it with hot glue or staples gun. Later we will form a pocket above this hand as if he keeps his hand in the pocket. It will look very casual and sailor-like. To indicate the pockets I suggest to mold bumps onto the trousers.

Jack the sailor - Material

Baseplate made from wood or
Alternatively feet made from plywood
Chicken wire
Strong wire
Wooden bars and screws
newspaper
sticky tape medium width
cardboard
papier-mâché
sandpaper

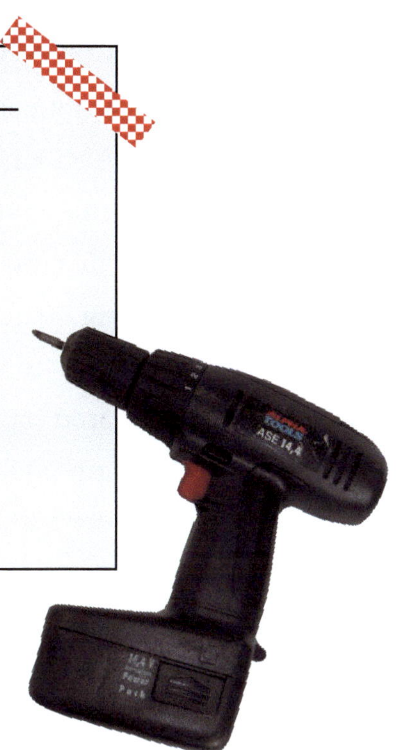

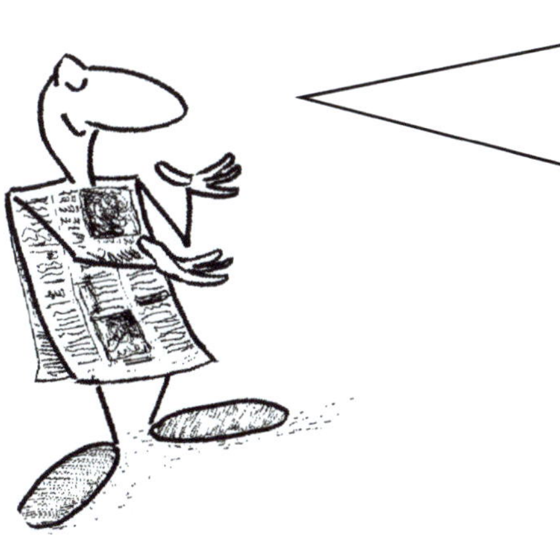

Sometimes I don't quite succeed in producing the perfect pulp. It is either too dry and crumbly or too liquid because I used too much glue. If you can't save your pulp by adding more paper or alter-natively water or glue, just use it as a first layer for another figure. Produce then new and better pulp for your current project and save the minor quality pulp in the fridge for the time being.

Adapting papier-mâché to any structure

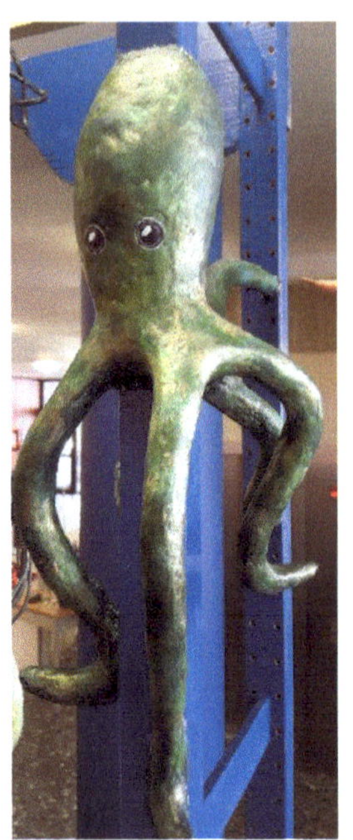

You may have noticed that some of the introduced objects were mounted on lampposts or roots. It is another advantage of this material, i.e. applying it to any structure is quite easy. Of course you will still need a carrying structure. It is important to attach it firmly to the structure that will have to be coated by papier-mâché. In the case of the lamp post you will initially wrap newspaper firmly around it and fix it with sticky tape. This will prevent the „filler" from rotating around the pole and you will be able to form the intended figure on it.

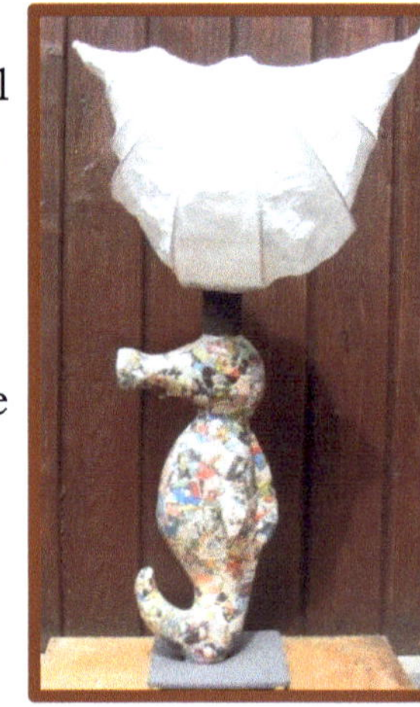

When you want to attach the figure to roots, wooden beams or treebranches I suggest to first build the raw design using meshwire, newspaper and strong wire. Fix the basic design to the wood by screws and the help of strong wire. Pulp will only be applied to the figure, once it sits on its final position on the lamp or root.

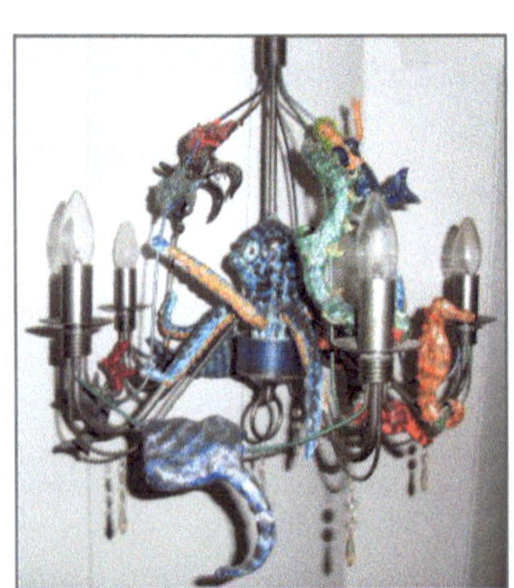

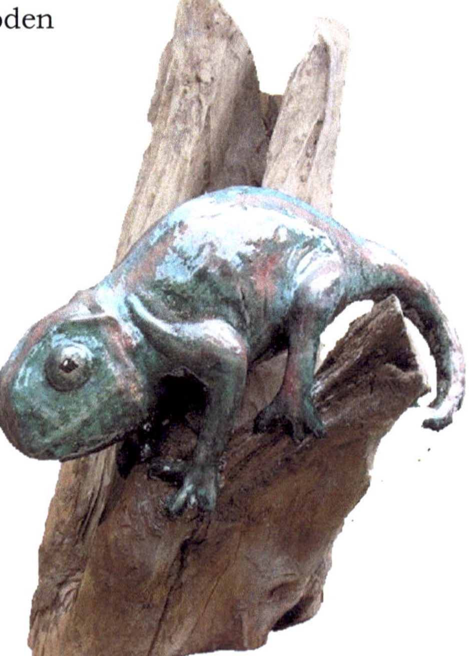

More examples of figures that have a complex inner framework

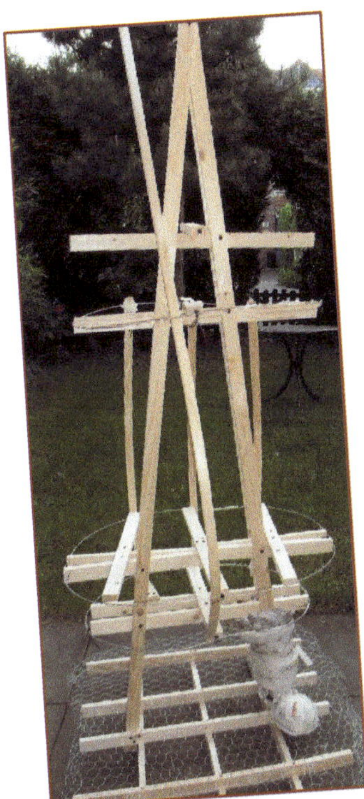

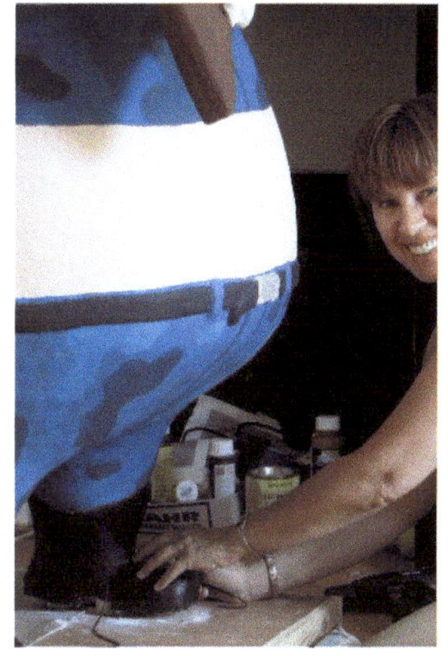

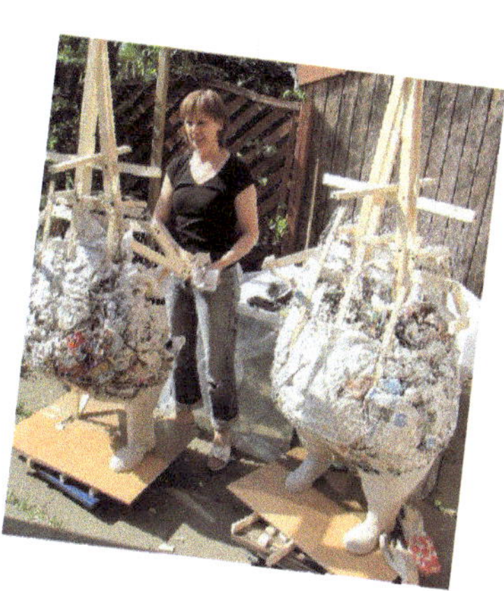

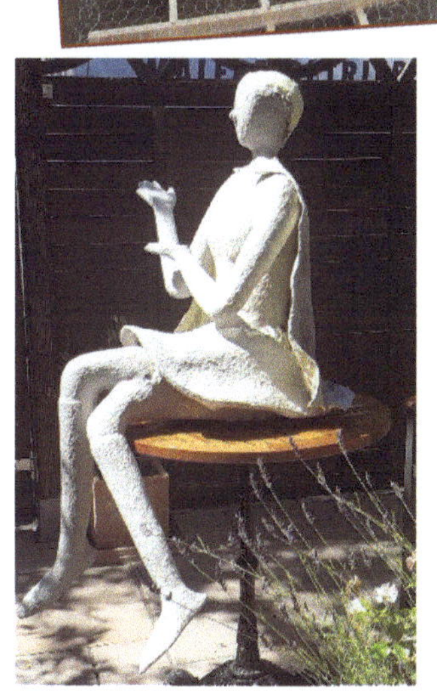

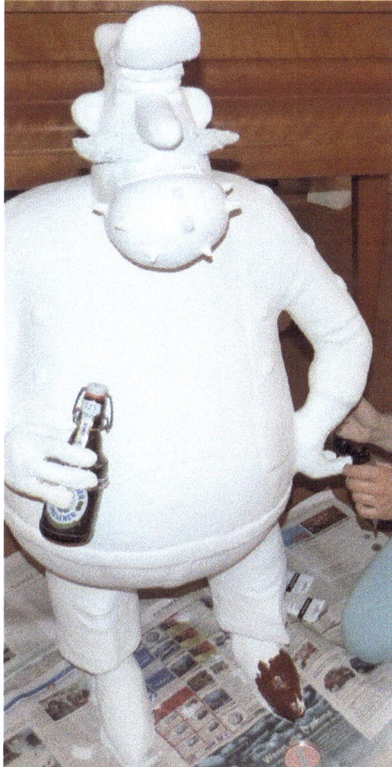

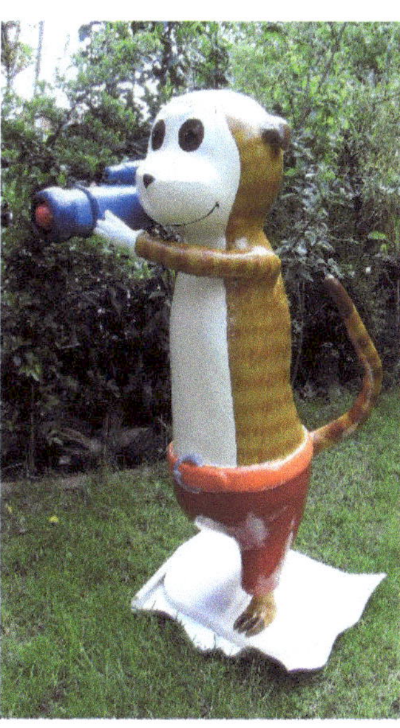

CHAPTER 6

Finishing

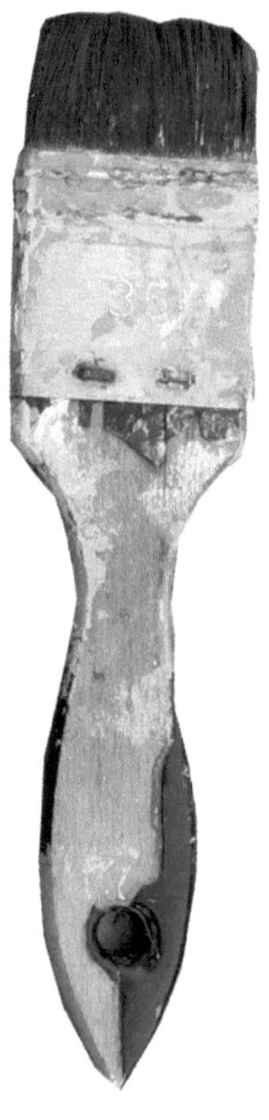

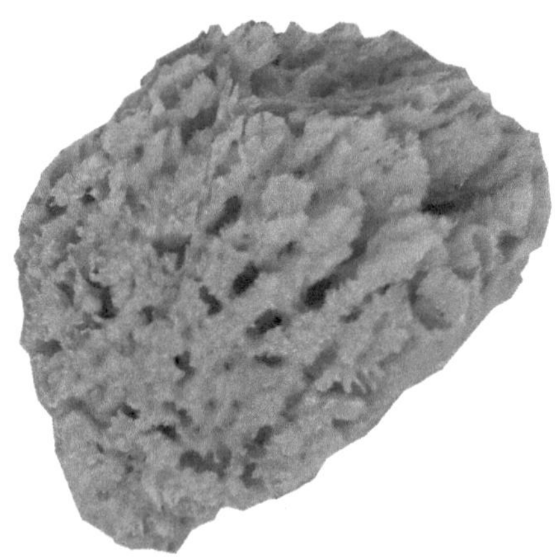

The dried surface

At first, when you apply the initial layer of pulp, your figure might appear flawless and smooth in its wet state. However, as it dries, the pulp tends to settle into the mesh and shrink slightly during the drying process, leaving the surface looking a bit uneven and textured. Once fully dried, the figure often takes on the classic rough appearance of papier-mâché, with small bumps where the fibers of the newspaper become visible as the 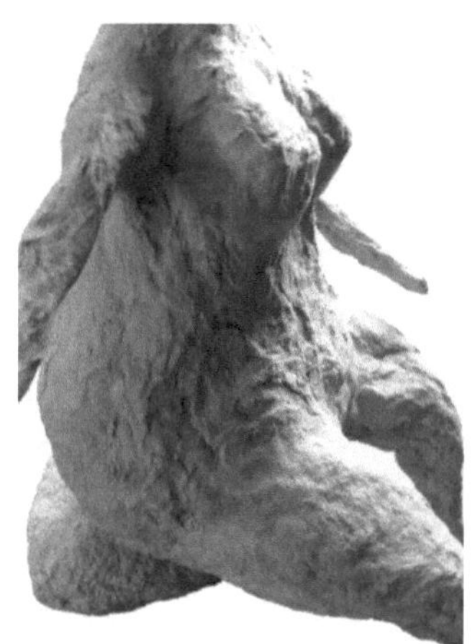 paste and moisture evaporate.The more effort you put into preparing ultrafine papier-mâché, the finer and smoother the dried surface of your sculpture will be. That said, not every project requires a perfectly polished look. The natural, slightly rough texture of traditional papier-mâché can be quite charming, especially for rustic or animal figures, where a touch of organic imperfection adds to the appeal.

For those who, like me, often prefer a sleek, smooth surface, achieving that finish requires a little extra patience—but it's absolutely worth it! If the initial layer of papier-mâché feels too uneven for your liking, simply apply a thin second layer using finely made pulp. This allows you to refine the design and surface, bringing your sculpture closer to perfection.

There are two main methods for smoothing rough surfaces: sanding and filling. Sanding helps to remove lumps, wrinkles, or glue marks, while filling smooths out any dips or crevices. Both approaches are effective and can be tailored to suit your desired finish. In the next chapter, we'll explore these techniques in more detail, giving you the tools to transform any textured surface into one you're proud to display.

Smoothing by sandpapering

Dried papier-mâché may be sandpapered just as wood. However, sandpapered papier-mâché makes the fibers stand up which we don't want. Therefore I suggest to varnish the sandpapered surface with Gesso (learn more later) and afterwards in a second step sandpaper the sticking out fibers (medium fine sandpaper 120-180 Grit).

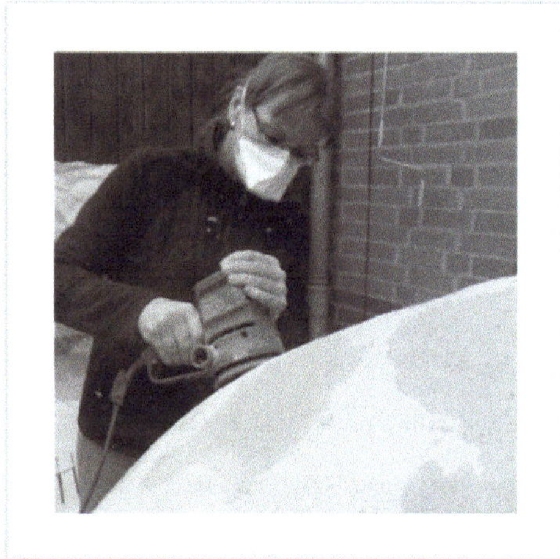

Depending on the envisaged impression this procedure might need to be repeated.

Thus treated papier-mâché can have the appearance of a lot of materials. Most visitors to my artist's studio are usually surprised that all exhibits are made by papier-mâché. Some look like wood carvings, others appear metal-like and yet others

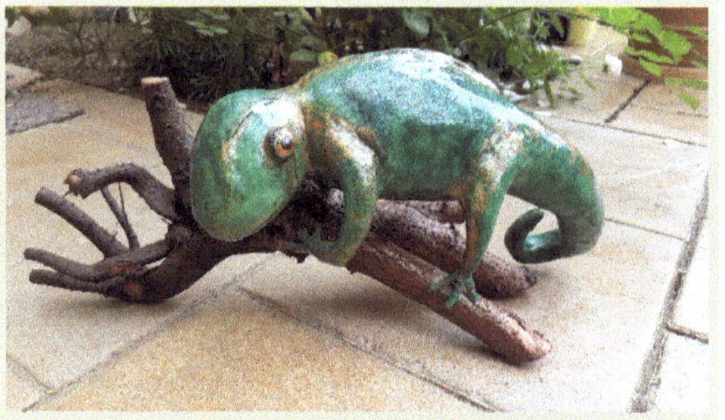

make you believe to be made of marble or china. It's all a question of surface treatment and painting/varnishing. Papier-mâché being so versatile enchants me still after so many years.

Smoothing applying layers of newspaper

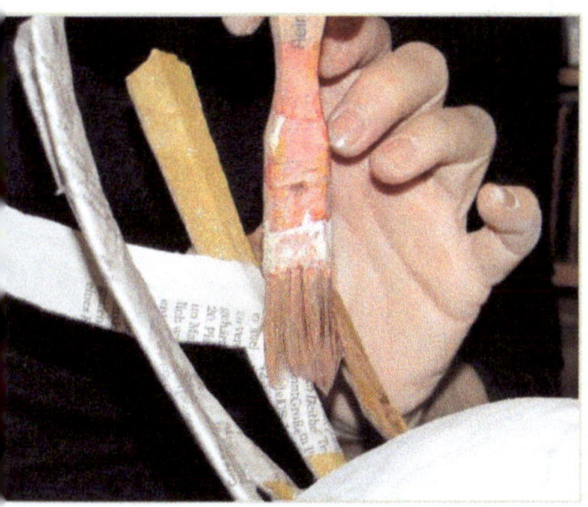

Once the figure is completely dry, you may want to create a more even surface by applying a finishing layer of newspaper strips. For a smoother result, start by spreading wallpaper paste onto a section of your figure, then carefully lay strips of paper onto it one at a time. Press each strip down gently with additional paste, ensuring it adheres well. Repeat this process by overlapping more strips and applying at least three layers in total. (When I use the term "figure," I refer broadly to all kinds of objects, including sculptures, pictures, or even furniture.) Please note that this method won't deliver a perfectly smooth surface, as the newspaper strips will naturally conform to the existing contours and textures of the object. However, after a few layers, the surface will feel noticeably smoother. For best results, use sturdier paper, such as wrapping paper, and tear it into smaller pieces by hand. The smaller the pieces, the more effectively they can adapt to the shape of the figure. Additionally, the more layers you apply, the stronger your piece will become.

When layering, alternate the direction of the strips—for example, lay the first layer horizontally and the second vertically, and so on. This alternating technique adds stability and ensures even coverage. If your figure includes rounded shapes, small bumps, or recessed areas, longer strips may not adhere easily. In such cases, switch to narrower strips that can better conform to curved surfaces without wrinkling. Once you have finished layering, any rough edges or overlapping rims can be smoothed down with fine sandpaper. If you desire an even smoother finish, you might consider using plaster materials for a more refined surface.

Plaster

To achieve the best result in smoothing the surface of the papier-mâché sculpture, consider applying an even finer or smoother substance to your project. I will introduce you to several options available at your local DIY store, outlining their advantages and disadvantages.

First, let's examine gypsum plaster commonly used for interior building work. It comes in powder form and is quite cost-effective. It can be applied using a scraper or even by hand (although using disposable gloves is advisable). After a short drying time, it can be easily sanded, resulting in a very smooth surface. To enhance water protection, consider using oil-based paints and waterproof varnish. One drawback of plastering the sculpture with gypsum is that it significantly increases its weight, making it very heavy depending on its size. Additionally, there is a limited window for correcting plaster work due to its rapid drying process.

Exterior filler compound

For more extensive projects consider using a slower-drying compound designed for exterior building work. This easy-to-mix powder can be applied with a brush (using more water) or with a scraper. Using a brush allows for more delicate coverage of parts like fingers, nose, and ears. Moltofill, once dried, can be easily sanded and is purported to be 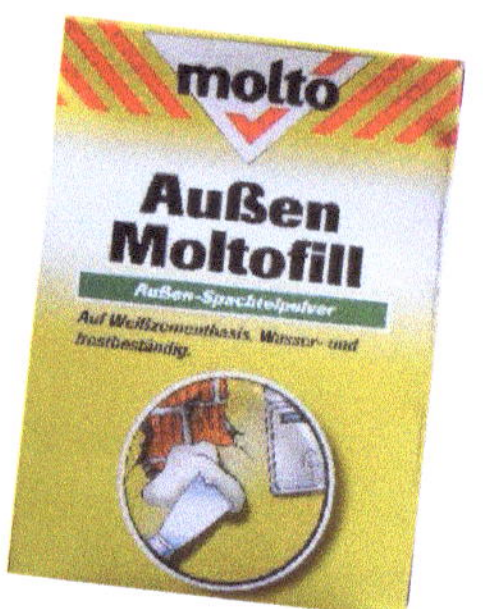 waterproof. Paint and other finishes can be applied according to preference. My personal experience with this material is limited to several sculptures that have been exposed to weather for five or six years, and they are still in good condition.

Air Dry Clay

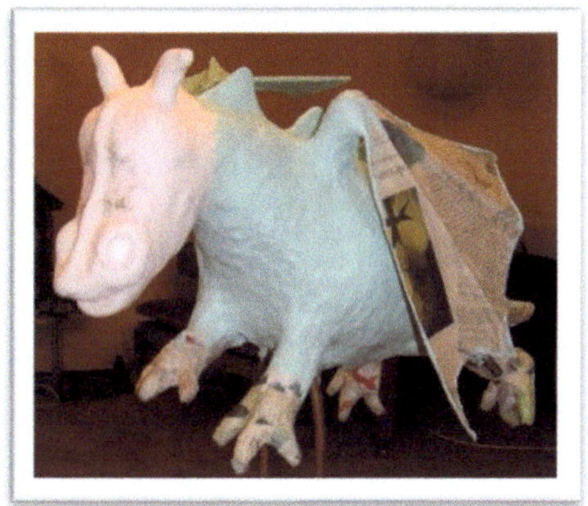

Your local DIY shop offers soft modelling self-hardening Air Dry Clay, which is my preferred material for smoothing the surface of my sculptures. It can be easily applied after kneading it with water until it feels smooth but not overly sticky. Use wet fingers to spread it into any dents until the surface is even. Alternatively, you can use a sponge or a knife with a flexible blade. After sanding, the surface will be perfectly smooth and ready for final treatment. However, be cautious: excessive filling may result in cracks on the surface during drying. One drawback of this material is its price, as it is relatively expensive – at least for large figures.

Acrylic Structural Paste

Acrylic plaster is another excellent material choice. While it hardens similarly to traditional plaster, it typically doesn't suffer from the same issues of cracking or breaking. To achieve a smooth surface, apply it with a slightly moist, almost dry sponge, working the material carefully into any folds, gaps, or uneven areas. After allowing the material to settle for a few minutes, smooth the surface using a moist sponge or your hands. For an even smoother finish, wait until the object is dry and repeat the process, beginning with another round of sanding. This material is also suitable for adding characteristic features to the surface, such as scars or wrinkles. To do this, apply a slightly thicker layer of acrylic plaster and then use a finger or a wooden stick, like a toothpick, to draw some material outwards, shaping lines or folds.

Pulp from Egg Cartons

Due to their recycled nature and the already crushed fibers Egg Cartons are perfect for creating an exceptionally soft papier-mâché pulp with optimal surface characteristics. Begin by soaking the egg cartons in water overnight, making label removal effortless the next day. Tear the cartons into small pieces and boil them in a large pot of water for approximately an hour. Then, use a hand blender to shred everything until you achieve a soup-like consistency. Boiling the cartons facilitates the easy dissolution of the fibers. Once cooled, strain this "soup" through a net or curtain and mix in glue (refer to page 17 for the "making of papier-mâché"). Apply this mixture in a thin layer over the entire sculpture using your fingers or a flexible knife. Personally, I prefer to reserve this substance for the final layer due to its perceived value. It yields a smooth surface while still retaining the characteristic qualities of papier-mâché.

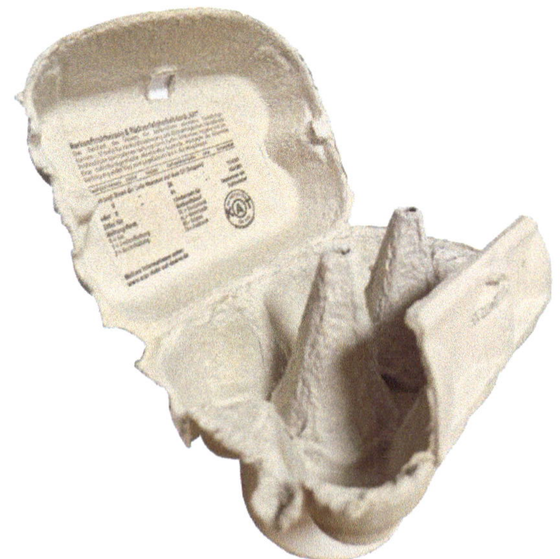

Gesso

Gesso is a mixture of chalk, calcium carbonate and pigment. It contains small particles filling up the pores and cracks on the surface of papier-mâché. For sculptures that need to be durable I apply several layers of Gesso onto the dried papier-mâché, sandpapering each layer before applying the next one. By this procedure the surface is hardened, is more durable and waterproof to a limited extent. Gesso is not too expensive and comes with the colors black or white, so that it is ideal for priming. Use white Gesso to brighten up the final colours.

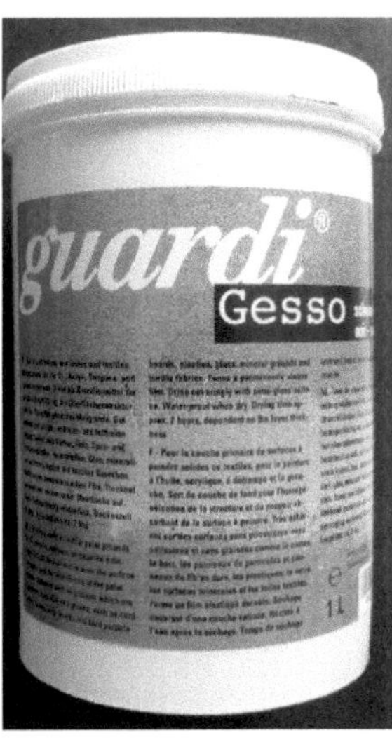

Black Gesso is perfect if you want to achieve a metallic impression. In that case apply a thin layer of metallic color and allow the black Gesso to shine through.

For those of you who are feeling a bit more adventurous, I'd like to share a "recipe" for making Gesso that I found online (though I haven't had the chance to try it myself yet)

1 unit gipsum chalk
1 unit zinkwhite pigment
1 unit animal glue

Apply Gesso like color with a brush.

Waterresistance of papier-mâché

Many of my workshop participants ask me whether papier-mâché is waterproof and if the sculptures can be placed outdoors. The answer is: papier-mâché itself cannot be waterproof. Even when glue is added, it remains a combination of shredded and glued fibers that swell when exposed to moisture. The only way to make a sculpture suitable for outdoor use is to seal its surface, meaning to coat it in such a way that rainwater cannot penetrate through the paint layer to the papier-mâché underneath. Papier-mâché reacts similarly to wood—it expands in warm temperatures and contracts when cold. This means the coating must be flexible, not rigid. A rigid varnish could crack when the sculpture contracts, whereas a polyurethane varnish is flexible and adjusts to the movements of the papier-mâché, helping to prevent cracks. Polyurethane varnishes are available in various finishes, allowing you to choose the look that best suits your project.

Laminating with Glue

Coat your sculpture with small pieces of sturdy packing paper, applying glue instead of paste this time. It is important to apply several layers, allowing each layer to dry completely for optimal protection. Once the sculpture is painted, apply multiple layers of a transparent PU varnish or an acrylic varnish suitable for outdoor use for additional sealing.

Filler or Primer

Another option is to smooth the figure with waterproof filler suitable for outdoor use, as described earlier. After this, apply two coats of outdoor acrylic paint to seal the surface.

Powertex Textile Hardener

Powertex, applied in two layers directly onto the dry sculpture, offers a somewhat pricier but quick solution for sealing papier-mâché. Originally designed for use on fabrics, this textile hardener can also be brushed directly onto papier-mâché. The advantage? After drying, the surface feels like plastic and becomes smoother. Make sure to use Powertex designed for outdoor applications to ensure waterproofing. Paint can be applied directly on top of the Powertex layer, followed by a protective varnish.

Epoxy Resin

Another reliable method involves using epoxy resin. This material forms a hard, water-impermeable layer after curing, effectively protecting your papier-mâché sculpture from moisture. However, care must be taken during application, as liquid epoxy resin can be hazardous to health. Be sure to work in a well-ventilated area and use proper protective gear, such as gloves and a respirator.

Concrete

Concrete and other mixtures requiring large amounts of water are generally unsuitable because they rewet the already dried papier-mâché layer. This can cause it to shrink and create cracks in the concrete surface.

Remember, regular inspections and maintenance will help extend the life of your outdoor papier-mâché sculptures. Check the coating periodically for cracks or signs of wear and repair as needed to ensure lasting protection. Whenever possible, avoid exposing your sculpture to frost, as frost can create tiny hairline cracks in the coating, which may allow water to seep in over time. I am constantly discovering new and improved methods for waterproofing papier-mâché, and I would love to hear your experiences as well! Feel free to share them with me at info@papiermache-kunst.de so I can include them in the next update of the book.

This garden dragon was coated multiple times by me. Initially, I used an exterior filler compound, followed by painting the figure with outdoor acrylic paint. On top of that, I applied a flexible acrylic clear coat. After all, this figure has survived about 7 years in my garden. That's pretty good, isn't it?

+   +   +   +   +

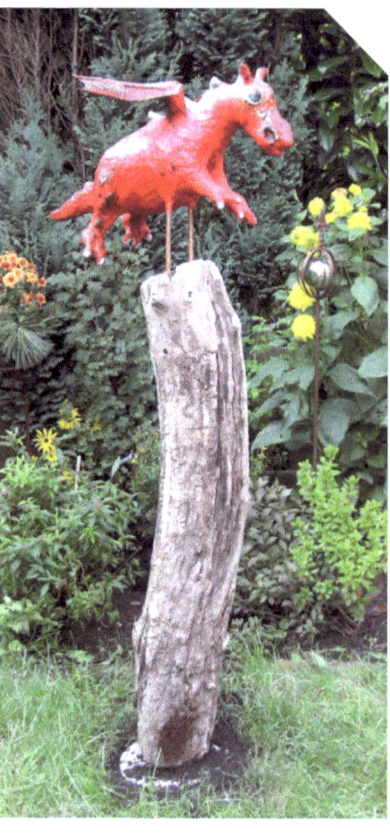

I hope you enjoyed this trip into the world of papier-mâché. You might not find each of the introduced sculptures appealing. However, they are prime examples for the framework you need for any sculpture you would want to create. You might have noticed, how important I consider the frame as a base for a sound and durable piece of art.

I hope I've managed to convey to you the same enthusiasm for using papier-mâché in your artwork as I have. I must confess that even after all these years of working with papier-mâché, I am still deeply fascinated by this material. I enjoy producing, kneading, and shaping it, using it to create my own personal pieces of art. I am confident that you will feel the same way too.

Please contact me for any questions: info@papiermache-kunst.de
Have fun!

Anke Redhead